MW01716084

ANGELS DEMONS & YOU

Unseen Spiritual Influences in Our Lives

© 2025 by Allen Jackson
ISBN 978-1-61718-083-5

Published by Allen Jackson Ministries™
P.O. Box 330128 / Murfreesboro TN 37133
allenjackson.com

All rights reserved. No part of this publication may be reproduced, stored in a retrieval system, or transmitted in any form or by any means—electronic, mechanical, photocopy, recording, scanning, or other—except for brief quotations in critical reviews or articles, without the prior written permission of the publisher.

All scripture quotations in this publication, unless otherwise indicated, are taken from THE HOLY BIBLE, NEW INTERNATIONAL VERSION®, NIV®. Copyright ©1973, 1978, 1984, 2011 by Biblica, Inc.™ Used by permission of Zondervan. All rights reserved worldwide. www.zondervan.com.

Other Bible translations represented and indicated in this publication:

ESV Scripture quotations taken from The ESV® Bible (The Holy Bible, English Standard Version®), © 2001 by Crossway, a publishing ministry of Good News Publishers. Used by permission. All rights reserved.

NASB Scripture quotations taken from the New AmericanStandard Bible®, Copyright © 1960, 1962, 1963, 1968, 1971, 1972, 1973, 1975, 1977, 1995 by The Lockman Foundation. Used by permission. www.lockman.org

NKJV Scripture quotations taken from the New King James Version. Copyright © 1982 by Thomas Nelson, Inc. Used by permission. All rights reserved.

NLT Scripture quotations marked NLT are taken from the Holy Bible, New Living Translation, Copyright © 1996, 2004, 2015 by Tyndale House Foundation. Used by permission of Tyndale House Publishers, Inc., Carol Stream, Illinois 60188. All rights reserved.

Printed in the United States of America

ANGELS DEMONS & YOU

Unseen Spiritual Influences in Our Lives

ALLEN JACKSON

TABLE OF CONTENTS

ABOUT THIS BOOK

This book was written from the transcripts of Pastor Allen Jackson's sermon series, ***Angels, Demons, and You***, which he delivered at World Outreach Church in Murfreesboro, Tennessee.

INTRODUCTION

Angels and demons exist.

Does that statement make you wince? Are you tempted to close this book because it broaches an idea that's uncomfortable or seems fanatical? Let's try this one:

Not only do angels and demons exist, but they also have a direct influence on *you*, all of the time.

Now I may be really pushing your comfort level, but I want you to be aware and prepared for the battle that's taking place all around us—the pressure is only going to increase. Ignoring the topic or saying, "I don't really believe in that," doesn't make it any less real.

There is a battle raging in the earth, and the authority behind it does not come from governments, constitutions, the United Nations, or any other institution. The origin is ultimately spiritual, and the Church has a role to play.

Ephesians, chapter 6, verse 12 says, "*For our struggle is not against flesh and blood, but against the rulers, against the authorities, against the powers of this dark world and against the spiritual forces of evil in the heavenly realms.*"

The essence of our struggle is not against flesh and blood; it's against the spiritual hierarchy—the Kingdom of God versus the kingdom of darkness. Whether we like it or not, we are engaged in that battle.

In this book, we are going to discuss angels, demons, and you—the word "you" is key. If we only talk about angels and demons, and we don't discuss their impact on you, this would become a theoretical discussion. If we're honest, those of us in the Christian Church are known for doing studies in a theoretical, distant sense, removing ourselves from the topic—as if it may or may not apply to us. It's like saying we want to talk about our health, but we only talk about diet and exercise on a surface level. But if we talk about diet, exercise, and *you*, it becomes much more personal.

In a similar way, it makes no sense to talk about angels, demons, and spiritual things and not include the implications for each of us, individually. My goal is to move beyond theological discussions to provide practical knowledge that can build your faith and make you stronger. I want you to be able to acknowledge the spiritual influences around you and be equipped to overcome whatever is ahead. We'll explore questions like:

- What does the Bible say about angels and demons?
- How do we recognize spiritual forces and their influence on us?

- How do we begin to see angels and demons as something as real as the people we encounter in our daily lives?
- How do we come alongside the angels, who work on behalf of God to bring about His good purposes on the earth?
- How do we actively diminish the influence of the demons, who are working to torment us and our families?

Being aware of the spiritual realm that exists around us is an extremely important component to being effective participants in God's Kingdom. As we begin, take a moment to ask yourself three foundational questions about the Word of God—which is the basis for this entire discussion:

1. How does Scripture impact my life right now?
2. What choices can I make to give it even greater authority in my life?
3. What do I currently believe about angels and demons, and am I willing to allow God's Word to inform those beliefs?

Pondering these questions in an honest way will provide the motivation to dig deeper into our understanding of God, His Word, His power, and what He has called us to do in His Kingdom.

Before we continue, it's important to recognize we aren't smart enough or strong enough to battle evil on our own. We need God's help. When we accept Jesus as Lord of our lives, we gain the spiritual authority to stand and fight against evil, through

Him. So, an important first step in this journey together is to take the time to read this prayer aloud, even if you have prayed it before:

Almighty God, I am a sinner, and I need a Savior. I believe Jesus is Your Son, and that He died on a cross for my sins. I believe You raised Him to life again for my justification. Forgive me of my sins. I forgive everyone who has sinned against me. Jesus, be Lord of my life. I want to serve You as Lord and King. I thank You that I now belong to the family of God. In Jesus' name, amen.

SECTION 1

THE UNSEEN REALITY AROUND US

01 CHAPTER ONE

ANGELS AND DEMONS EXIST

When we talk about angels, demons, and spiritual things, I realize I'm inviting you toward something that might be beyond the arenas you have considered before. What I'm really asking you to do is to imagine there is a substance to our faith beyond membership in a church or visiting the same location every Sunday morning. We need to expand our imaginations and learn to see the world through God's eyes—not our own—so we're prepared to engage in the spiritual conflict around us. God has more He wants to show us, but we need to be willing to see it.

Feeling some resistance toward this topic is a normal response. We tend to build our lives based on what is familiar and what we've learned in the past. I'd like to offer some new pieces of understanding that will help you be more fully aware and better prepared as a Christ-follower. Our world is changing, and we need to be ready for whatever is ahead. That means we need to open ourselves more fully to the Lord and His Spirit, so we can understand how to serve Him in this specific season.

It's tempting to stay anchored in what we've always known, but Jesus Himself shows us what happens when we close our hearts to spiritual things. In Matthew, chapter 13, Jesus had begun His public ministry in Capernaum, located on a busy road along one of the major fresh water sources of the ancient world. Capernaum was a place with enormous traffic, and if you wanted to establish a reputation or had a message to be communicated, it was a good location to be. But Jesus left Capernaum to return to His hometown of Nazareth, a sleepy little village tucked away in the hills of Galilee:

> *Coming to his hometown, he began teaching the people in their synagogue, and they were amazed. "Where did this man get this wisdom and these miraculous powers?" they asked. "Isn't this the carpenter's son? Isn't his mother's name Mary, and aren't his brothers James, Joseph, Simon and Judas? Aren't all his sisters with us? Where then did this man get all these things?" And they took offense at him. But Jesus said to them, "A prophet is not without honor except in his own town and in his own home." And he did not do many miracles there because of their lack of faith.*
>
> MATTHEW 13:54-58

This passage offers a short but poignant story. Jesus probably knew the people in that community better than those in any of the other villages He visited. He was more familiar with the synagogue in Nazareth than any other He ministered in—it was His home synagogue. He knew the stories of the people who were occupying the seats because He had grown up there. Yet when He comes to Nazareth and begins to teach from Scripture, the people didn't say His teaching was wrong, heretical, or incorrect. Instead, they were offended by His insight and understanding. They were put off by Him. They said, "We know Him. We know His family, and we know His siblings. Just precisely who does He think He is?"

It's the outcome documented in verse 58 that most intrigues me: *"And [Jesus] did not do many miracles there because of their lack of faith."* That's the idea I want to hand you to reflect upon. You see, their familiarity with Jesus limited their imaginations.

I think we have a bit of that challenge. Our familiarity with Christianity and our comfort with spiritual routines and habits limits our imaginations. We fall back on thoughts like, *We haven't done that before*, or *We've never seen God do that*, or *I'm not really sure about what you're saying.*

But our world is changing. Your cell phone has more computing technology than the computers that landed the astronauts on the moon's surface several decades ago. While the fundamentals of our faith have not changed, we're going to have to grow in our faith to meet the challenges of this new season. The stability of the world we live in has shifted, and we need to get to know God and His Kingdom in a better way.

In Nazareth, selfish ambition blinded the people to Jesus. They were so focused on what made sense to them, feeding their pride and their view of the world, they didn't recognize God was doing something new through Jesus. They may have thought, *That's Joe's son. Our kids went to school with his kids. Why does Jesus suddenly think He's better than us?* There's a lot of that type of skepticism and arrogance in the background of this story. In a similar way, if you don't guard your heart, your selfish ambition will keep you in a place of unbelief. You can't dare believe God or listen to Him because you might have to turn loose of some of your own ambitions. You'd have to invite God into the midst of your life plan—and if we're honest, we might think, *I just really want God to bless my life. I don't want Him meddling with it.*

The people in Nazareth rejected who God had sent to them, and when they did, they forfeited a great deal. So, before you decide what you don't believe, or what you won't believe, or "that's not the way I grew up," I want you to be aware that, in choosing not to believe, you can forfeit much of what God would bring to you.

So, throughout this book, I encourage you to open your heart and begin to say to the Lord, "Lord, I want to see the world from Your perspective more clearly than I ever have before." Before you read on, let's pray that right now:

Heavenly Father, help me to see myself, the people around me, the world, and Your Kingdom from a perspective that's more fully aligned with You and Your Word. Give me eyes to see, ears to hear, and a heart to embrace the new things You will show me. In Jesus' name, amen.

Now, open your Bible, open your heart, and begin to seek the Lord and get to know Him in a new way. He's an infinite God, and we are finite creatures. If you learn something new about God every day for 100 years, there will still be more to learn about Him at the end of that 100 years than all you've learned before. I've become quite comfortable taking the posture of a beginner. Beginners get some latitude—and if we have the attitude that we're all beginners, we'll be positioned to continue to learn our entire lives!

We need to become comfortable learning new things because God's directives for our lives are often opposite to what our culture teaches. Our society leads us to believe that our physical attributes (strength, beauty, financial condition, education, race, IQ, and social status) determine our life outcome far more than spiritual influences. This extends into the Church's culture, as well. We say we're Christ-followers, and we believe the Book, and we believe in Jesus, and we've made some efforts around that. But we spend the majority of our time, energy, and effort investing ourselves in all these other things, as if they are far more significant. We become far more emotional about them. When we discuss spiritual things, we start backing up and growing nervous. This is not a criticism. We've all been in that place! If we acknowledge where we are, we can find our way out of it.

To create a solid path forward, we need to understand how we got to this place where the Church is so spiritually unaware—because the Church hasn't always been like this. The twenty-first century Church, particularly in the West, is not reflective of the Church in every century. We've lost a little perspective and drifted a bit.

How did we get here?

I think a significant contributor is the way we have approached biblical studies for several decades now: biblical criticism. Biblical criticism is a school of thought that uses critical analysis to explain the Bible. It's a technical application that leads you to unpack the background of the story to find the real meaning of the text. I spent a good bit of time in university settings being trained in how to do this. So, it's not a theory to me.

Biblical criticism is broken down into several categories (which are constantly morphing and changing), including textual criticism, literary criticism, source criticism, form criticism, and redaction criticism. There are entire theology schools built around this approach to biblical studies. Decade, after decade, after decade, we've trained Church leaders in this way—and this isn't something subtle or small. It defines the biblical worldview of a significant percentage of people engaged in the contemporary Church in our nation and in the Western world.

Tragically, the outcome of biblical criticism is to imagine that the Bible is little more than an epic human effort—albeit a remarkable one, spanning broad periods of time, with enormous influence. They say the Bible is worthy of study, but it shouldn't be understood to have a divine component or influence. Instead, with biblical criticism, the point in reading and studying your Bible is not faith, or belief, or application; it's to dissect or study God's Word as if it's inert—not alive, vibrant, and transformational. They say that if you begin to attribute more to it, you've drifted beyond the realm of logic and may be on the lunatic fringe.

Just for the record, I don't accept the premise of biblical criticism. I believe that approach is faulty, and it has led many in the Church to an unfruitful destination.

It's important to remember that biblical criticism is not the only school of thought regarding Scripture, nor does it reflect the attitude of the early Church or the Church through most of its history. Biblical criticism is very much a latecomer to biblical studies, but it is very prevalent in this season. It informs much of the dialogue that's held in some of the most celebrated expressions of faith today.

That's why it feels easy to dismiss conversations about angels and demons—the first century audience believed in those things, but we're in the twenty-first century. We say, "We haven't been trained that way. We've studied the social context and the historical context." We act as if, somehow, we're a bit more enlightened and more aware. We're a bit too sophisticated to believe in things like the Devil. That attitude leaves us tremendously vulnerable, and that's why this study of angels, demons, you, and me, is important.

Let's start out with some big-rock ideas that we'll discuss in depth in the pages ahead:

Spiritual Forces Influence History

I earned a degree in history, and I think knowing history is enormously valuable. But at this point in my life, I have reached the conclusion that spiritual forces are probably the greatest single determining factor in the outcome of history—more than technological innovations, economic booms, and political parties.

Spiritual Forces Are Important

We see the spiritual forces in the opening chapters of Genesis, and their interactions with humanity fill the pages of our Bibles through the book of Revelation (the story of the conclusion of this age), but we often read past it. Without supernatural interaction, Jesus' birth would not have occurred. It's safe to say that this historical event changed the unfolding story of humanity, and the spiritual world introduced that change.

Spiritual Forces Still Impact Our World Today

When the gospel came to the city of Ephesus, it made such a

dramatic change in peoples' hearts that it disrupted the economic patterns of the city. Wouldn't it be amazing to see this kind of spiritual change transform the hearts of men and women across our nation? What if that spiritual shift impacted our patterns of living so much that the economic repercussions caught the attention of the ungodly? What if we didn't need to boycott a company as a means of punishment, but they began to see a need to adjust their products and marketing patterns because of a shift in our living habits that affected their bottom line?

Spiritual Beings Exist All Around Us

The unseen realm contains spiritual beings in significant number.

There are good spiritual beings. God's angels are ministering spirits and messengers sent forth to help us. They fill the pages of Scripture, and yet we tend to imagine they are peripheral or secondary—that you can be a Christ-follower and not really have to think about the angels and all they do for you and God's Kingdom. You don't want to worship them, and it doesn't make you more spiritual to know their names, but they are there to help you!

There are also bad spiritual beings. Satan and the evil beings that serve him oppose God and anyone who stands for Him and His Kingdom. When Satan was cast out of Heaven (see Luke 10:18), a third of the angels rebelled and went with him, and he rules over them. The Bible also talks a great deal about demons, unclean spirits, and evil spirits—they're synonymous, interchangeable terms, depending upon translation or the place where they're used. Their intention is to destroy the things of God—including you and me.

It's good to remember that Satan was defeated through Jesus' death, burial, and resurrection. We live in the victory that Jesus accomplished, but we have not been delivered from the battlefield. That's why in Ephesians, chapter 6, we're told to put on our armor and to do everything we can to take our stand against the Devil's schemes. We can't overcome evil on our own. We need God's help.

We Can Influence the Spiritual Realm

It's important to recognize the magnitude of the spiritual forces because you and I have the opportunity, with our voices and our lives, to address those spiritual forces and influence them.

Not thinking about this reality doesn't protect you. Just as godly spirits can influence your life, so can unholy spirits. We have rather naively tried to say, "I'm a bit too sophisticated to believe in the Devil." Well, I wish we could be so sophisticated we didn't have to believe in viruses, but the reality of them has nothing to do with sophistication—they still make you sick.

We Must Allow Scripture to Inform Us

As we begin this study, don't simply accept my opinion. I'm not the judge. Also, don't just form an opinion. Work to have an informed opinion—not just a position based on the church you grew up in or a grandparent's idea—but an opinion grounded in Scripture.

Take the Word of God and begin to study it for yourself. Allow it to challenge what you believe, as the Holy Spirit reveals new things to you. Ask God to deepen your understanding of the spiritual forces that impact your life, so you can be equipped to diminish the impact of the enemy and live as an increasingly powerful influence for His Kingdom in every place He leads you.

LET'S PRAY

Almighty God, forgive me for my unbelief and indifference. I humble myself and acknowledge You as the Creator and Sustainer of all things. Now, open my heart and my eyes that I might have understanding and insight from You. Deliver me from deception. Holy Spirit, teach me. I am listening, and I will follow. Give me a boldness to believe, to serve, and to respond as never before. May the name of Jesus be lifted high, and may His people be strengthened. In Jesus' name, amen.

02 CHAPTER TWO

THE ROLE OF ANGELS

Did you know you could interact with an angel and be completely unaware? Hebrews 13, verse 2 says, "*Do not forget to show hospitality to strangers, for by so doing some people have shown hospitality to angels without knowing it.*" You won't necessarily hear their wings flapping, and you won't have to put on your sunglasses because of the glow of their halo, but you could find yourself in the presence of an angel at any time.

The Bible tells us many more things about angels:

- They are ministering spirits.
- They are guardians.
- They are messengers.
- They encourage and protect.
- They execute God's discipline and judgment.

- They are spiritual beings.
- They are not limited to time—they didn't get an "earth suit" like you and me.
- They are far more prevalent in our realm of existence than we typically realize.
- They move between dimensions. They interact with you and me in time, and yet they're creatures of eternity. Our "earth suits" make us creatures bound to time, but our spirits are eternal. You see, eternity is not just a long, long time; it's a completely different realm of existence. Angels are active in both the realm of time and eternity.

This is a lot to take in, so we'll start by discussing a point that directly impacts us today: Angels are ministering spirits sent to help us—the people who believe in Jesus.

Angels Are Ministering Spirits

Hebrews, chapter 1, verse 14 says, *"Are not all angels ministering spirits sent to serve those who will inherit salvation?"*

"Salvation" refers to the redemptive work of Jesus: His death, burial, and resurrection. Jesus made it possible for any human being who will choose Him as Lord, and turn from their sin, to experience a new birth into the Kingdom of God and be made a totally new creation. The word we typically use for that experience is "salvation," and the Bible says all the angels are ministering spirits sent to help and serve those who will inherit salvation—that's you and me!

It's important to recognize that the redemptive work of Jesus on the cross was not intended to help any of the angels who rebelled against God—they aren't going to get saved. The Devil is not going to make a profession of faith. God's angels are ministering spirits sent on *our* behalf! They are here for *our* benefit, and that makes me smile. If you invest as much time thinking about angels as you spend thinking about the bad news, it will change your worldview.

If God has provided ministering spirits to help us, maybe we should know a little bit about them, who they are, and what they're about. Angels are not weak, harp-playing onlookers—they are mighty in strength, and they are busy doing what the Lord has instructed them to do.

Psalm 103, verses 19 and 20 say, "*The LORD has established his throne in heaven, and his kingdom rules over all. Praise the LORD, you his angels, you mighty ones who do his bidding, who obey his word.*"

As we continue this study, we'll examine the magnitude of the presentation of angels and their strength, influence, and abilities. The language the Bible uses to describe them is truly phenomenal.

Angels Are Guardians

There are several examples of how angels are sent to us as guardians. Genesis, chapter 3, verses 23 and 24 say, "*So the LORD*

God banished [Adam] from the Garden of Eden to work the ground from which he had been taken. After he drove the man out, he placed on the east side of the Garden of Eden cherubim and a flaming sword flashing back and forth to guard the way to the tree of life."

Cherubim is one of the classifications of angels. In Hebrew, that "*im*" ending is plural. Cherubim and seraphim are part of the created beings. Usually, they're described to us when we see pictures of the throne of God and the creatures surrounding God. But in this case, these heavenly beings were given an assignment to guard the Tree of Life.

In Exodus, chapter 14, we're also given a clear display of angels as guardians. Exodus is the story of how the Hebrew slaves were delivered from Egyptian slavery, and it was not an easy deliverance.

If I told you God delivered me from some horrific place, you might imagine it was easy, joyful, and happy—that I skipped merrily along with no problems or challenges. But many of you have read the book of Exodus, and you know that the Israelites' story of deliverance was beyond difficult. There were many stresses, points of unbelief, and opportunities for questioning. There was anger about leadership, resentment over what was happening, and a lot of fear. In Exodus, chapter 14, we see one snapshot of this struggle, and it takes place after the Passover. The Hebrews had been released from slavery, but then Pharaoh changed his mind. He gathered his chariots and his army and set out after the former slaves.

Exodus, chapter 14, verses 19 and 20 say, "*Then the angel of God, who had been traveling in front of Israel's army, withdrew and went behind them. The pillar of cloud also moved from in front and stood behind them, coming between the armies of Egypt and Israel. Throughout the night the cloud brought darkness to the one side and light to the other side; so neither went near the other all night long.*"

Pharaoh caught the Hebrews, and it says the angel of the Lord stood between them—that part is quite clear. But it's hard for me to imagine that the Hebrews had a standing army, since they had been slaves for hundreds of years. One of the titles attributed to the Lord is "The Lord of Hosts." If you read *The Message* (which I realize is not a translation, but bear with me), every time you see "The Lord of Hosts," *The Message* translates that as, "The Lord of the Angel Armies." Now, *the angel army* isn't specifically mentioned there in Exodus, but it does say the angel of the Lord was present. I imagine that the angel of the Lord took up his position along with the heavenly host, darkened the perspective of the Egyptians, and brought light to the Hebrews. The angels intervened and changed the course of history!

Angels are guardians, and you have angels watching over you right now. The Bible clearly talks about guardian angels who carry out God's directions and do God's bidding. And they are still in the earth today, right where we live and work, doing God's business and watching over you right now!

It's also good to know there are angels assigned specifically to children. In Matthew, chapter 18, verse 10, Jesus says, *"See that you do not despise one of these little ones. For I tell you that their angels in heaven always see the face of my Father in heaven."*

Imagine all the angels attached to all the children. Think about that the next time you treat a child unfairly. We will be harshly judged if we turn our children over to wickedness, immorality, and ungodliness. Very few things in Scripture bring a response from God more quickly than abandoning children to wickedness.

Angels Intervene

We find an interesting angelic intervention in Numbers, chapter 22, which tells us about Balaam, a man who is not all good but also not all bad. He's aware of spiritual things, but he's also very carnal, greedy, and selfish. The hardest characters in life are in those groups. They'll worship the Lord with enthusiasm and behave in an ungodly way with great enthusiasm, too. Don't be one of those people. You could miss the Kingdom of God.

If it's hard for you to imagine that God would send an angel to intervene in the life of a disobedient person, look at what happened to Balaam. Scripture says a ruler recognized the threat the Israelites presented and wanted them to be cursed, so he hired Balaam. He was paid a lot of money to pronounce a curse on the Israelites as they traveled between Egypt and the Promised Land.

God told Balaam not to go, but he ignored God, and the angel of the Lord stood in the road to oppose him. Here's the ironic part: Balaam didn't recognize the angel—his donkey did! The donkey had more discernment than he did! The donkey saw the angel standing in the road with a drawn sword in his hand and turned off the road into a field. Balaam beat the donkey to move her back on the road.

Then, the angel of the Lord stood in the narrow path, and to avoid the angel, the donkey pressed close to the wall, crushing Balaam's foot against it. If you have ever ridden a horse or a donkey, that may have happened to you. They'll rub your leg against a tree or the wall in the barn. The Bible says Balaam beat the donkey again. Then, the angel of the Lord moved on ahead and stood in a narrow place where there was no room to turn, so the donkey laid down.

If you've ever worked with donkeys, this is a very accurate description of donkey behavior. Our church had a donkey for a while. We used to take part in our local Christmas parade, and we wanted our section to feature Mary, Joseph, and a burro. So, we bought a little burro, and we named him Murphy—Murphy burro—which is kind of cute when you live in a town named Murfreesboro. We brought him into the church, and I had the privilege of training Murphy to come in and out of the building. I worked for weeks, training the donkey to walk in and out of the church door like he was walking in and out of his stall, going to be fed. I thought he was good to go, but it didn't occur to me that I also needed to train Mary and Joseph. They didn't know how to stand up to his unruly temperament. Things didn't go well. So, Christmas was donkey-less that year. I tell you all of this because when Balaam's donkey laid down, I know exactly what that's like!

The story gets better. Numbers, chapter 22, verse 28 says the Lord opened the donkey's mouth and she talked! She said to Balaam, *"What have I done to make you beat me these three times?"* Instead of being bewildered by the fact that his donkey was suddenly talking, Balaam answered her! In verse 29 he said, *"You have made a fool of me! If only I had a sword in my hand, I would kill you right now."*

Balaam was clueless. He had no idea the bad behavior was the donkey's reaction to the angel of the Lord, who was carrying out God's direction.

Finally, the Lord opened Balaam's eyes, and he could see. It's important to note that God gave Balaam multiple opportunities to repent of his stubbornness, rebellion, persistent wickedness, and pure greed. The pursuit of money was causing him to set aside God's direction and essentially say, "It doesn't matter to me." But ultimately, this story shows how angels can intervene—even through a donkey—to redirect man's plans and bring about God's purposes.

Angels Deliver God's Judgment

This leads me to the next important role angels hold: They are instruments of God's judgment. In 2 Samuel, chapter 24, David took a census of the soldiers, even though God had told him not to do it. Disobeying God always brings bad consequences, and God sent word through a prophet that He was going to discipline David. The catch was that David had a choice: The discipline could come through other men or through God Himself. David chose the option that was dependent upon God's actions, and not the actions of other people, saying, "I trust God to be more merciful than my enemies."

We see the punishment begin in verse 16, which says, *"When the angel stretched out his hand to destroy Jerusalem, the LORD relented concerning the disaster and said to the angel who was afflicting the people, 'Enough! Withdraw your hand.' The angel of the LORD was then at the threshing floor of Araunah the Jebusite."*

The threshing floor of Araunah the Jebusite is a place that holds a significant role in the Bible. It is known historically as Mount Zion and Mount Moriah, which is where Abraham brought Isaac to offer him as a sacrifice. It's where Solomon would build his Temple, and where the Second Temple in Jerusalem would be built by Zerubbabel. It's where Jesus would teach and minister in the courtyards. When you look at pictures of Jerusalem today, you'll see a gold-domed building, which is a Muslim shrine to Muhammad—but it is resting on a platform built by Herod the Great—and that's the same place where we find this angel.

The Lord was grieved because of the calamity, so He said to the angel, "Withdraw your hand."

We find David's response to the angel's destruction in verse 17. He says to the Lord: *"I have sinned; I, the shepherd, have done wrong. These are but sheep. What have they done? Let your hand fall on me and my family."*

This is a clear example of God using His angels to orchestrate the beginning and end of someone's judgment and discipline.

Isaiah, chapter 37, shows us a different historical account of how angels are instruments of God's judgment. The Assyrians, with their superior military might and technology, had come to conquer Jerusalem, and there was no chance the people in Jerusalem could defend themselves. King Hezekiah prays in desperation. Then, the prophet Isaiah sends a message to Hezekiah telling him the Lord heard his prayer, and he did not need to worry. We see why in verse 36: *"Then the angel of the LORD went out and put to death a hundred and eighty-five thousand in the Assyrian camp. When the people got up the next morning—there were all the dead bodies!"* God sent His angels to defend Jerusalem that night. The Assyrian men who remained in the morning didn't continue the attack—they departed in a hurry. Hezekiah prayed, and God moved on his behalf, accomplishing what Hezekiah and his people could not do.

There is a lesson for us in Hezekiah's story. We live with increasing fear of people and decreasing respect and reverence for God. Our spiritual lives have been so anemic and small. Our spiritual awareness is so limited. We've relegated our faith to studies, groups, events, and theological debates. Our willingness to believe is so dwarfed that we struggle to imagine that God is involved in the history of human beings—and yet we see examples of this throughout the Bible.

We need to cultivate the imagination that God is actively engaged in our lives. As we continue our study on the roles angels have in our world in the next chapter, we'll see more biblical examples of how God sends spiritual beings to help us, encourage us, protect us, and communicate with us. They are ready to demonstrate God's strength and judgment on our behalf. We are not alone, and we have not been abandoned!

LET'S PRAY

Heavenly Father, thank You for Your angels and for the assistance they've brought us, even without our awareness. Thank You that nothing is hidden from Your sight, and You know all things. Lord, I ask You to help me see and understand the spiritual realm in new ways. Give me the courage and boldness to learn, grow, and follow You as I move forward. In Jesus' name, amen.

03 CHAPTER THREE

ANGELS ENCOURAGE AND PROTECT US

We've all had moments when we were at the end of ourselves and completely spent—emotionally, physically, or spiritually—with nothing left. I have some good news: God will intervene in those moments of desperation by sending angelic messengers to help. We see several examples of this in the Bible, and one of my favorites comes from studying the life of Elijah.

Elijah lived in a time when God's people ignored the Word of God. They were killing prophets and practicing paganism. Elijah was one of those prophets, and he exuded strength and authority as he held up God's truth in the midst of a culture that didn't want to hear it.

One of Elijah's most dramatic moments came when he literally called fire down from Heaven, killing the prophets of Baal and hundreds of idolatrous, false prophets. To say his actions made the people mad would be an understatement. In 1 Kings, chapter 19, we find brave, bold Elijah afraid and running for his life. After traveling a long way south into the desert, he came to a broom tree, sat down under it, and prayed that he might die. "I've had enough," he said, "Take my life. I'm no better than my ancestors." Then, he laid down under the tree and fell asleep.

Suddenly, an angel touched him (an angel touched him!) and said, "Get up, eat something." He looked and found bread and a jar of water. So, he ate, drank, and went back to sleep. Then, the angel of the Lord came back a second time, touched him, and said, "You need to eat some more because the journey is too much for you."

Here's what I want you to notice: At the point where Elijah was so exhausted emotionally, physically, and spiritually that he said, "I can't do it anymore. Lord, I'm done," God sent an angel to help him. And the help came in a very practical, tangible way: food to eat. Do you think angels are still doing that today? I do!

We're similar to Elijah because we've been called to represent God and our biblical worldview to a culture that often doesn't want to hear our message. Are we willing to persevere, or will we withdraw because it's too difficult? When you're tempted to imagine our faith is about always being kind or timid, think of

Elijah calling down fire from Heaven—that's a bold response!

People actively standing for their faith is a significant theme throughout Scripture, and we're called to do this in our generation. This doesn't mean you should be violent or angry. But it's time to recognize there's more in the balance. The outcomes of our actions (or our failure to act) are significant. We've spent our lives thinking we could secure our futures with the resources available to us, so we've lacked a sense of urgency when it comes to following the Lord. Instead, we tend to think of spiritual things as being kind of trivial—maybe a little scary—and certainly on the periphery of someone with our intellectual ability. It's time to align our beliefs with what we find in Scripture. And that includes what the Bible says about angelic beings.

Let's get back to Elijah—there's something else we need to learn from his story. In 2 Kings, chapter 1, a group of soldiers came for him. Do you think he was afraid? He had plenty of reasons to be! But God knew what was going to happen ahead of time, and He prepared Elijah by sending comfort to him through an angel who said in verse 15, "Go down with the soldiers. Don't be afraid." So, Elijah got up and allowed the men to take him to the king.

This is another great example of God sending angels to prepare His people and to help them when they are frightened of their circumstances. His angels are still busy doing similar things right now.

The faith and experience of the people who have come before us can help strengthen us today. A significant portion of the Old Testament—Psalms, Proverbs, and even passages in the prophets—deals with lessons people learned along their journey and makes it clear the Hebrew people understood angels had a significant involvement in their history. These stories were written down—not only as historical references—but to encourage the following generations (that's you and me!). When we read these accounts, it helps us understand the role of the angels and how those same angels continue to minister to God's people today.

Angels Protect Us

Angels not only encourage and help us, they protect us! We find an example of the angels' protection in Psalm 34, verse 7, which says, *"The angel of the LORD encamps around those who fear him, and he delivers them."* This passage offers great motivation for cultivating the fear of the Lord. When we respect and revere God, it attracts angelic involvement. What a promise!

We see what it can look like when angels come to our defense in Psalm 35, verse 1: *"Contend, LORD, with those who contend with me; fight against those who fight against me."*

It continues in verses 5 and 6: *"May they be like chaff before the wind, with the angel of the LORD driving them away; may their path be dark and slippery, with the angel of the LORD pursuing them."* The next time someone stands against your faith, imagine them on a dark and slippery path with the angel of the Lord coming for them. That's a path I wouldn't want to be on!

A prophetic book that offers several examples of angels protecting God's people is the book of Daniel. Daniel was thrown into the lion's den in Daniel, chapter 6. Verse 22 says, *"My God sent his angel, and he shut the mouths of the lions. They have not hurt me, because I was found innocent in his sight."* God protected Daniel from ravenous lions! Once again, we see that angels protect us.

The story of Daniel's faith and his willingness to stand for God continues. In chapter 10, God shows Daniel a vision of a great war, and he mourned and fasted for three weeks. As he was standing on the banks of the Tigris River, an angel came to him. Their conversation is recorded in chapter 10, verses 12 and 13: *"'Do not be afraid, Daniel. Since the first day that you set your mind to gain understanding and to humble yourself before your God, your words were heard, and I have come in response to them. But the prince of the Persian kingdom resisted me twenty-one days …'"*

When the angel says, "the prince of the Persian kingdom," he isn't talking about an earthly prince but a spiritual prince. A spiritual authority of darkness over the Persian kingdom delayed the angelic messenger from reaching Daniel—that's a spiritual battle!

The Scripture continues, *"'Then Michael, one of the chief princes, came to help me …'"* Michael is one of the archangels, and his primary assignment is ministering to the Jewish people, including Daniel. Verse 14 says, "*'Now I have come to explain to you what will happen to your people in the future, for the vision concerns a time yet to come.'*"

Here's a quick recap of what we just saw: Daniel began to intentionally seek the Lord, and God sent an angel. When the angel couldn't get to Daniel because of an evil spirit, the Archangel Michael stepped in to help. So, not only did God send one angel to help Daniel, but He also sent an archangel with a greater level of spiritual power and authority. Can you see why we will not defeat evil by outworking it, out-thinking it, or out-organizing it? It's not about our numbers. The only thing evil will yield to is a power greater than itself. That power isn't represented in our physical strength or our monetary assets; that power is represented in the King of kings and the Lord of lords. We, the Church, have to be aware of the power that's available to us through Jesus.

God sent an angel in response to Daniel's prayers, and our choices can also attract an angelic response from God. This isn't just an abstract or whimsical idea. Our God-choices impact God's choices toward us. I'm sorry we haven't been coached in this better. We've been coached to be born again and then to not lie, cheat, or steal. But if you seek God and pursue Him earnestly, He will respond to you.

What Do We Do Next?

Now that we're beginning to recognize these truths about angels and the spiritual realm, what will our response be?

Our trip through time is relatively brief. The Bible says we're like flowers, here today and gone tomorrow. Yet our time under the sun with an earth suit is enormously significant for our role in eternity. Your earth suit has a countdown clock. It will run down. But when our body physically dies, we're not done. Our spirit steps into eternity. The point of our days under the sun is to invest our time and talents in efforts that impact eternity.

So, let's ask the Lord to begin to open our eyes. I don't mean just to see angels and the spiritual forces at work in our lives, but to open our eyes to His reality and His truth. We want to go beyond the habits of Bible study, or attending worship services, or being good, polite, or tame. Those things are great and necessary, but there are real issues in our lives where we need the power of God to bring about acceptable outcomes, and God's responses aren't whimsical or arbitrary. We need our eyes to be opened! Luke, chapter 24, says Jesus opened His followers' minds so they could understand the Scriptures, and He will do that for us, too!

In Acts, chapter 16, Paul was directed to Philippi supernaturally in a dream. When he arrives, one of the people listening to him speak was a woman named Lydia. She was a dealer in purple cloth from the city and a worshiper of God. The Lord opened her heart to respond to Paul's message. The Lord Himself opened her heart—and He will respond if we ask Him to open ours.

This doesn't have to be complicated. Offering simple little prayers will change the trajectory of your life. Just begin to say, "Lord, open my heart. I don't want to just sit in church and leave my faith there. I don't want to try to defend myself. I don't want to try to defend what I think is right and excuse what I think is wrong. I don't want to be a debater with You, God. Open my heart. Give me a longing for the things of Your Kingdom." God will respond to you.

In John, chapter 20, verses 21 and 22, we find Jesus with His disciples on Resurrection Day. He said, *"'Peace be with you! As the Father has sent me, I am sending you.' And with that he breathed on them and said, 'Receive the Holy Spirit.'"*

One more idea I'd like to offer you, as we open our hearts to new spiritual topics, is to begin to say to the Spirit of God, "You're welcome in my life. I'm not as familiar with You as I'd like to be. I don't really recognize Your voice. To be honest, I'm a little frightened of the topic. I don't know You as well as I'd like to know You. Would You help me?"

The best way that I know of to attract the involvement of the Holy Spirit is to give honor to Jesus. If you'll commit yourself to honoring Jesus, speaking well of Him any place you go, you take Him with you. Don't go any place where you're not willing to bring Jesus. If you honor Jesus, the involvement of the Holy

Spirit in your life will increase in a dramatic way, and He will reveal new things to you.

LET'S PRAY

Heavenly Father, I joyfully yield my life to the Lordship of Jesus. Through Him, I have been freed from the kingdom of darkness and brought into Your Kingdom of light. Through Jesus, I have overcome the enemy. Give me the strength and courage to complete the course You have chosen for me. Fill my heart with joy and help me to see You and Your plans for me more fully than ever before, that my life would make a difference in eternity. In Jesus' name, amen.

SECTION TWO

ANGELS IN THE BIBLE

04 CHAPTER FOUR

JESUS AND HIS ANGELS

There is no Jesus-story without angelic involvement. So, if you think you're going to complete your God-assignment without angelic assistance, that idea did not come from Scripture.

We see angels present throughout the story of Jesus: before His birth, during His lifetime, after the resurrection, and after He ascended into Heaven. Throughout each of these phases, angels are not only present, but they also play an integral role.

In this chapter, we'll look at Jesus' life in time—that span of thirty-three years while He was living with us in the earth—and how the angels were involved at every point.

An Angel Visits Zechariah

Even before Jesus' birth as a baby, the angels were preparing for

His arrival. In Luke, chapter 1, we meet Zechariah, who was a priest at the Temple in Jerusalem. The priests served by rotation, and when it was his turn to serve, verses 11 and 12 say, "*Then an angel of the Lord appeared to him, standing at the right side of the altar of incense. When Zechariah saw him, he was startled and was gripped with fear.*"

Meeting an angel was not an everyday occurrence—it startled Zechariah! As we read on, we see that this eternal, spiritual being talked to Zechariah in a way he could understand. That means angels are multilingual—it's good to know!

The story continues into verse 13, "*But the angel said to him: 'Do not be afraid, Zechariah; your prayer has been heard. Your wife Elizabeth will bear you a son, and you are to call him John.'*"

Zechariah and Elizabeth were childless, and they had been praying for a child. The angel came to announce that Elizabeth was going to conceive, and verse 18 says, "*Zechariah asked the angel, 'How can I be sure of this? I am an old man and my wife is well along in years.'*"

What captures my attention is the response from the angel—who happened to be Gabriel—in verses 19 and 20. Gabriel, an archangel, is one of the most powerful angels. "*The angel said to him, 'I am Gabriel. I stand in the presence of God, and I have been sent to speak to you and to tell you this good news. And now you will be silent and not able to speak until the day this happens, because you did not believe my words, which will come true at their appointed time.'*"

Remember, Psalm 103, verses 19 and 20 say, *"The LORD has established his throne in heaven, and his kingdom rules over all. Praise the LORD, you his angels, you mighty ones who do his bidding, who obey his word."* Angels perform God's Word, and they obey the voice of His Word. We see Gabriel doing this with Zechariah.

In our parenting classes at our church, one of the principles we teach is first-time obedience. The aspiration for parents is that your children cooperate the first time they hear the invitation, not the twelfth. Similarly, God expects first-time obedience from us.

When the angel came to visit Zechariah, he didn't know if the angel was Gabriel or Fred. He had no discernment and no recognition. The angel didn't have a name tag, and nothing about the angel's presence suggested he was unique in any way. So, when Zechariah questions Gabriel's message, Gabriel basically says, "Do you know who I am?" Zechariah answers, "No, I really don't." Gabriel responds, "Well, I am Gabriel, and I stand in the presence of God, and because you didn't believe it, you're going to be quiet for a while." When Zechariah came out of the Temple, he was mute until nine months later, when his son was born. Luke, chapter 1 says they asked Zechariah for his baby's name, and he wrote "His name is John" on a tablet. Then, verse 64 says, *"Immediately his mouth was opened and his tongue set free, and he began to speak, praising God."*

That little interaction helped Zechariah believe!

The Angel Visits Mary and Joseph

But Gabriel was not done:

> *In the sixth month of Elizabeth's pregnancy, God sent the angel Gabriel to Nazareth, a town in Galilee, to a virgin pledged to be married to a man named Joseph, a descendant of David. The virgin's name was Mary. The angel went to her and said, "Greetings, you who are highly favored! The Lord is with you."*
>
> LUKE 1:26-28

The Christmas narrative is familiar to us, but the role of the angel in the emergence of Jesus into time is significant. In fact, if I were going to give you a big-picture perspective at critical moments in the unfolding story of God throughout Scripture, the angels are involved at those pivot points. When there is a need for a message to be communicated with such clarity, and such specificity, and it is beyond the normal routine of expectations, the angels are involved.

In Matthew, chapter 1, verse 19, we see Joseph's response to Mary's news of the miraculous conception of Jesus: *"Because Joseph her husband was faithful to the law, and yet did not want to expose her to public disgrace, he had in mind to divorce her quietly."*

Why does Joseph have that attitude when Mary was pregnant,

and there was no way he was the father? You and I would tell him, "She's pregnant because of the Holy Spirit," but that would be hard for anyone to believe at that moment—let alone a couple of teenagers. They had no peer support. There was no literature on the topic to help them navigate their way through.

Verses 20 to 21 continue, *"But after he had considered this, an angel of the Lord appeared to him in a dream and said, 'Joseph son of David, do not be afraid to take Mary home as your wife, because what is conceived in her is from the Holy Spirit. She will give birth to a son, and you are to give him the name Jesus, because he will save his people from their sins.'"*

Joseph would have missed the God-opportunity before him without the help of an angel. His wife's pregnancy represented a breach of trust, and there was no explanation that could have bridged that gap other than a message from beyond time; there was certainly no explanation in time.

Angels Announce Jesus' Birth

Angels were also involved at the announcement of Jesus' birth. This is an important premise. We need to understand that the angels are often involved in announcements, preparing the current generation for what God is doing in that season.

We see that angelic role in the book of Luke:

> *And there were shepherds living out in the fields nearby,*

> *keeping watch over their flocks at night. An angel of the Lord appeared to them, and the glory of the Lord shone around them, and they were terrified. But the angel said to them, "Do not be afraid. I bring you good news that will cause great joy for all the people. Today in the town of David a Savior has been born to you; he is the Messiah, the Lord. This will be a sign to you: You will find a baby wrapped in cloths and lying in a manger."*
>
> LUKE 2:8-12

It sounds so romantic, but I've fed animals a good chunk of my life, and where you put the grain and the hay for livestock is not a place you want to put a newborn. Trust me.

The story continues:

> *Suddenly a great company of the heavenly host appeared with the angel, praising God and saying, "Glory to God in the highest heaven, and on earth peace to those on whom his favor rests." When the angels had left them and gone into heaven, the shepherds said to one another, "Let's go to Bethlehem and see this thing that has happened, which the Lord has told us about."*
>
> LUKE 2:13-15

The angels are celebrating because Jesus has stepped into time, and it was good news for all people! The Messiah had come to the earth, but I want to pause and note that Jesus has been involved with humanity since the beginning.

You see, one of the mistakes we make is we think of Jesus as only having a thirty-three year engagement with humanity. Most of us think of Jesus as a New Testament character, but I would submit to you, that's a bit simplistic. It's illogical to me to imagine that the Savior of all humanity, the Redeemer of all humankind, has nothing to do with the initiative between God and human beings until we get to the Roman Empire. Yes, He was born in Bethlehem, crucified in Jerusalem, then ascended to Heaven during that time. And in Acts, chapter 1, Jesus stepped into that little portal of time and interacted with us again. But Scripture shows us that Jesus has been engaged with humanity from the opening of Genesis, and His involvement continues to the conclusion of the story.

The Bible tells us how to know the Creator of Heaven and Earth, and how to be prepared for our lives beyond time. The character who is the linchpin—the decision point in the whole narrative from Genesis to Revelations—is Jesus. And angels were the ones who announced His arrival into time.

Angels Protect Jesus

When the wise men departed in Matthew, chapter 2, verse 13, it says "*... an angel of the Lord appeared to Joseph in a dream. 'Get up,' he said, 'take the child and his mother and escape to Egypt. Stay there until I tell you, for Herod is going to search for the child to kill him.'*"

As I mentioned in earlier chapters, the Bible tells us that angels are involved in protection and security. Our contemporary word would be "intelligence," like the CIA (not IQ). Angels give you information your adversaries don't intend for you to have. They are ministering spirits sent to serve those who are the beneficiaries of salvation, and during Jesus' earliest years on earth, an angel appeared to Joseph and said, "You're going to need to move."

We need to reconcile some things in our minds. God was capable of orchestrating a virgin birth and directing wise men from the East to Bethlehem, a little insignificant village on the outskirts of Jerusalem. So, it seems like He would be able to foil Herod's plans and keep him from murdering those children. But that's not the pathway God chose. God chose to send Joseph some inside information and say, "You're going to need to move because they're coming for the boy."

We get a little choked up sometimes because we think we know how we want God to work and what we want Him to do. We dictate how the Creator of all things should engage with our lives, but that's not the paradigm the Bible presents. Instead, it says that you and I are to offer ourselves as living sacrifices to God. We are to do His will. So, if God tells you to move, don't ask Him to fix the problem while you remain stationary.

A little further in the story, Matthew, chapter 2, verses 19 and 20 say, *"After Herod died, an angel of the Lord appeared in a dream to Joseph in Egypt and said, 'Get up, take the child and his mother and go to the land of Israel, for those who were trying to take the child's life are dead.'"* The angel completes the circle, providing protection and security from beginning to end.

This should speak an important truth to us today: We benefit from angelic participation. They protect us and bring strength and renewal to us, just as they did for Jesus!

Angels Bring Jesus Help

Later, after Jesus' baptism, the Spirit led Him into the wilderness where He fasted and prayed for forty days. At the end of that time, the Bible says Jesus was hungry, and Satan himself came to tempt Him. Matthew 4, verses 10 and 11 say, *"Jesus said to him, 'Away from me, Satan! For it is written: "Worship the Lord your God, and serve him only."' Then the devil left him, and angels came and attended him."*

There is no Jesus-story without the angels' help. Do you think you're going to finish your God-story without angelic help? Do you think you're more clever, more discerning, more powerful, or wiser than Jesus?

Many of us have so much affluence, so many resources, and so many things to help us, it's easy to imagine that God could be just a complementary component of our lives. But you can't afford that if you believe your life has a God-assignment. You see, it's not just your life—it's the life God has entrusted to you, and offering it back to Him is your gift to Him. To complete our God-assignments, we're going to need some angelic assistance.

God sends angels to minister to us in difficult times, and if you ever doubt this fact, consider how they helped Jesus on the night of His betrayal. On His final night, Jesus was in Gethsemane, praying and desperate. His friends were of no help—they didn't even have the courage to stand with Him through the evening, and Jesus knew it. We find Him alone in the Garden in Luke, chapter 22, verse 42, when He says, *"Father, if you are willing, take this cup from me; yet not my will, but yours be done."* An angel from Heaven appeared to him and strengthened him.

This scripture reminds us that angels bring strength and renewal to our lives when we find ourselves in desperate situations. We're in a season right now where people are exhausted emotionally, physically, and spiritually. It's not an easy time. We need to understand there are resources available for our renewal and our strengthening. The next time you are at the end of yourself, with nowhere to turn, ask God to send His angels to help.

Angels at Jesus' Death

In Matthew, chapter 26, verses 50 and 51, we find a little window into the capabilities and the availability of the angels. Jesus was in Gethsemane: *"Then the men stepped forward, seized Jesus and arrested him. With that, one of Jesus' companions reached for his sword, drew it out and struck the servant of the high priest, cutting off his ear."* That was Peter who cut off the servant's ear, God bless him. They were coming to arrest the most remarkable man he'd ever known, and the best Peter could do was an ear.

The story continues in verses 52 and 53: *"'Put your sword back in its place,' Jesus said to him, 'for all who draw the sword will die by the sword. Do you think I cannot call on my Father, and he will at once put at my disposal more than twelve legions of angels?'"*

In the Roman military, a legion was anywhere from 3,000 to 6,000 soldiers, and it says there were *twelve* legions at His disposal. Jesus could call thousands of angels—they were ready and available. As excited as they were to announce His birth in the shepherds' fields outside of Bethlehem, don't you think they were ready at that moment, too? Don't you think Gethsemane would have been different if they had intervened?

But Jesus said, "I have to do this."

Suppose Jesus got to Gethsemane, and He said, "Look, I just don't really want to do this. I've led a sinless life, a perfect life, an obedient life. I've been rejected in the villages and the synagogues of this nation. I've been repudiated by the religious leaders, and I've done my part. This is more than I want. I'm at a point in my life where I'd rather relax." He wouldn't have fulfilled His assignment, would he?

We aren't the Messiah, but God has an important assignment for you and me, too.

If you think I'm doing an injustice to the context, I'll take you back to the Exodus generation. They were delivered from the brick pits of Egypt and taken to the boundaries of the Promised Land—their inheritance—and they said, "We just don't want to do it. It's too hard." The Bible tells us God was angry with them and said, "You'll die in the wilderness." And they did.

You see, I don't think it's appropriate to receive the blessings of God, the power of God, the deliverance of God, and all the things that God brings to our lives, and then say to Him, "Well, wait a minute, this is just a little harder than I want it to be."

But on more than one occasion, I've said to the Lord, "If the path has to be this difficult, I'm not sure I want to walk it." In my imagination, when I signed up to serve the Lord, I thought I would yield to Him, and He would pour His blessings out on me with such abundance they would crush me. The truth is, the Lord has blessed my life. He's been good, kind, and gracious to me in ways beyond any imagination or expectation I held. But I would also tell you that following the Lord has taken the very best I have.

If you've never thought of giving God your very best, I invite you to begin to think about that—because when we talk about angels, demons, and spiritual influences, this is not casual. You see, God can't entrust you with insight, discernment, and awareness until you've chosen to take Him seriously. It's the same as how we don't entrust children with things that will harm them. We don't let them handle scissors until they know how to use them safely.

I'm an advocate for hard work and good planning. That's not evil, wicked, or ungodly. But all the planning in the world doesn't take away the fact that we still need God's help. As we continue to explore some of these topics and themes, begin to quietly say in your heart to the Lord, "I'd like to know You better. I don't like all my circumstances. I don't necessarily like everything happening to me, but I would like to know You better. God, I've been pretty indifferent. I've tried to secure my future in my own self and my own strength."

Angels at Jesus' Resurrection and Return

After Jesus died on the cross, the angels were also involved with the Resurrection events. Matthew, chapter 28, verse 2 says, "*There was a violent earthquake, for an angel of the Lord came down from heaven and, going to the tomb, he rolled back the stone and sat on it.*"

I don't think God needed an angel to roll back the stone. The earthquake could have shaken it out of the way, but I think the angels wanted a roll! (This is my opinion. It's not in the text. You can disagree with me!) I think they had watched Jesus be crucified, and they wanted to engage in the next chapter, maybe saying, "Let me move the stone! I'd like to at least look at those soldiers guarding that tomb." I bet they never forgot their expressions!

The story continues:

His appearance was like lightning, and his clothes were white as snow. The guards were so afraid of him that they shook and became like dead men. The angel said to the women, "Do not be afraid, for I know that you are looking for Jesus, who was crucified. He is not here; he has risen, just as he said. Come and see the place where he lay."

MATTHEW 28:3-6

Can you feel the electricity rippling through Heaven? Thousands, upon thousands, upon thousands of angels are saying, "He's back! Just as He said!"

Matthew, chapter 28, continues into verse 7: "*'Then go quickly and tell his disciples: "He has risen from the dead and is going ahead of you into Galilee. There you will see him." Now I have told you.'*"

Where is Jesus, after He has risen from the dead? First Peter, chapter 3, verse 22 says, "*[Jesus] who has gone into heaven and is at God's right hand—with angels, authorities and powers in submission to him.*"

Jesus is in Heaven, but the angels—the messengers, those who are ministering spirits on our behalf—are in submission to our Lord and King, our great High Priest. You better believe He's engaged in what's going on in the earth today, and that the angels are doing His bidding. They're His messengers sent on His behalf so the purposes of God would come forth in our generation. We can't afford to say, "Well, I just don't know if I believe in all of that."

Matthew, chapter 16, verses 26 to 27 say, "*What good will it be for someone to gain the whole world, yet forfeit their soul? Or what can anyone give in exchange for their soul? For the Son of Man is going to come in his Father's glory with his angels, ...*" If you conquered the world and everything in it, it's going to look like a shabby representation of nothing compared to when you see Jesus return to Earth in all the glory of the Kingdom of God.

Time and again, Jesus links His return to this gathering of angels that are coming with Him. They've been so engaged in the story, from the beginning to the conclusion, that when it's time for the conclusion of this Age, they have pivotal roles to play.

More Angelic Interventions

We are often so unaware of the presence of angels, but that hasn't always been the story of the Church. There have been seasons in the unfolding story of the Church where God's people—the believers on Earth—understood they needed the help of angels.

In the book of Acts, it was an angel who walked into the prison to lead Peter out. Peter was going to be executed the next day, and an angel came and rescued him.

It was an angel who showed up to see John in Revelation, chapter 1, and said, "I have a message for you of what's coming."

It was an angel who visited Daniel when he was a slave in Babylon and said, "You are highly valued by God. I brought you some information."

I happen to believe we are at the beginning of the culmination of the Age, and we're going to need all the help available to us.

In Matthew, chapter 13, Jesus taught a parable about the wheat and the tares. We typically refer to it as "the wheat and the weeds," but the word that is used in Greek suggests a specific weed that looked like wheat—when you looked at the fields, you couldn't really distinguish between the grain you were trying to grow and the weeds that had intruded, competing for resources. So, it's not talking about godly people and the pagans. I think He's talking about all of those who say they follow Him.

The disciples privately asked for the meaning of the parable, and He responds:

> *"The one who sowed the good seed is the Son of Man. The field is the world, and the good seed stands for the people of the kingdom. The weeds are the people of the evil one, and the enemy who sows them is the devil. The harvest is the end of the age, and the harvesters are angels. As the weeds are pulled up and burned in the fire, so it will be at the end of the age. The Son of Man will send out his angels, and they will weed out of his kingdom everything that causes sin and all who do evil. They will throw them into the blazing furnace, where there will be weeping and gnashing of teeth. Then the righteous will shine like the sun in the kingdom of their Father. Whoever has ears, let them hear."*
>
> MATTHEW 13:37-43

Again, we see angels active in the earth. We need to open our hearts to that reality. Jesus didn't leave us alone when He ascended to Heaven in Acts, chapter 1. At the End of the Age, the angels are going to be integrally involved with the purposes of God coming into time. (We will discuss this at length in the next few chapters.) But angels are also here to help us now. We're not alone. Spiritual forces are real. They're as real as a virus that we don't see, and as we realize this, we find an opportunity.

We Need the Holy Spirit's Help

Now that we know angelic forces are real and we have seen their impact and roles in the Bible, let's begin to ask how to open our lives so we can cooperate more fully with them. We also need to ask how we can separate ourselves from the spiritual forces that would diminish or hurt us. We want all the help that is available to us, and the word that seems to best suit our response is "invitation." We want to be certain that we have given the Spirit of God a complete, wholehearted, unreserved invitation to help us and bring us support. Does that seem reasonable?

There are a number of ways to walk toward that, but I would encourage you to just begin by quietly saying, "Holy Spirit, You're welcome in my life." Then, just stop right there. Don't put any reservations. Don't define it by a specific expectation, or the lack thereof. Don't point at an experience you had and say, "Well, because I speak in tongues, I know everything about the Holy Spirit there is to know." Embrace the fact that we're all learners. Stop with the limits!

If you'll begin to exalt Jesus and honor Him, the Holy Spirit's engagement in your life will change. If you're ashamed, embarrassed, reluctant, or timid about Him, or if you trust the other resources in your life more than you trust Jesus, you are creating a very narrow opening for the Spirit of God to cooperate with you.

Recently, I've been singing this little song we learned as kids: "Jesus loves me, this I know, for my Bible tells me so." I haven't gotten much further than that. I just go over and over that little verse because it changes everything. You see, it doesn't have to be complicated. God doesn't need my IQ. He just needs me to yield.

I believe if you'll begin to yield, exalting Jesus in the practical ways of your life and consciously inviting the Holy Spirit in, He will bring you an awareness of spiritual things you will be amazed you've been overlooking.

The Church has been spending way too much time focusing on the darkness, threats, and challenges. Jesus wasn't worried about who came to arrest Him in the Garden. He didn't care how good they were with clubs and spears. He wasn't frightened because Peter was a little clumsy with his sword.

Instead, Jesus said, "Do you understand the resources I have? These clowns have no chance. I will go with them." He went with them and yielded Himself to them. It was their pride, arrogance, and pomposity that caused them to think they won when they arrested Jesus, but it was Jesus who won the victory over death in the end. For us to experience victory, too, we need to become increasingly more aware of Who is for us and what is at work on our behalf. Angels were at work throughout Jesus' life on earth, and they are ready and available to help us today.

LET'S PRAY

Almighty God, forgive me for my unbelief and indifference. I humble myself and acknowledge You as the Creator and the Sustainer of all things. Help me to see Your truth in a new way. Holy Spirit, deliver me from deception. Give me a new boldness to believe, to serve, and to respond as never before. May the name of Jesus be lifted high, and may His people be strengthened. In His name, amen.

05 CHAPTER FIVE

ANGELS IN REVELATION

The world around us will come to an end someday, and in the book of Revelation, John gives us details of what that will look like. It sounds like a frightening piece of fiction, full of doom and destruction, but it actually offers Christ-followers the very best news: Our Boss is coming back, and He's bringing the bonus checks!

Jesus gave us the outline for the book of Revelation while He was on Earth. In Matthew 16, verses 26 and 27, He said, "*'What good will it be for someone to gain the whole world, yet forfeit their soul? Or what can anyone give in exchange for their soul? For the Son of Man is going to come in his Father's glory with his angels, and then he will reward each person according to what they have done.'*"

In the passage above, Jesus Himself gave us the synopsis for the End of the Age: The Son of Man is returning to Earth, in His glory, with all of His angels, and He's going to reward each person for what they have done. This means Jesus will be the judge. But do we believe it?

As we look at Revelation, my goal isn't to unpack the entire book for you but to show you how angels will play a central role in the End of the Age. This doesn't mean that they played a lesser role through all of history. Angels visited Mary, Joseph, Gideon, Daniel, and other people who were present at pivotal, critical points in history. In the same way, angels are going to play a key role at the End of the Age. As we near the end, the curtain is pulled back a bit so we can be prepared and have enough insight to understand and flourish in our roles and assignments.

Angels are mentioned in every chapter of Revelation, except three. In two of the chapters where they're not mentioned, there's a lengthy description of the heavenly beings that surround the throne of God. The one chapter where they're conspicuously absent is chapter 13, which is focused on a description of the Beast.

Angels hold such a prominent place in Revelation that we're going to take the next several chapters to walk through the book and examine the angels' unique roles and assignments. It will help us understand how God reveals Himself to us, how He brings about changes in the earth, and what we can expect as we move closer to the End of the Age.

In the opening lines of Revelation, chapter 1, God gave Jesus the revelation of the End of the Age for one purpose: so He could make it known to His servants. God communicates this message through an angel.

Remember, the Bible tells us God's angels are messengers, ministering spirits sent on behalf of those who are inheriting salvation. So, when Jesus was given this portrayal of the End of the Age, He used one of His messengers to make it known to John. Without the angels, we wouldn't have the book of Revelation.

Once you see the significant role of angels in Scripture, I hope you'll move past the internal debate on whether they exist or not, and whether spiritual things influence our lives or not. There is a blessing that comes from believing the things of God. Revelation, chapter 1, verse 3 assures us of this when it says, *"Blessed is the one who reads aloud the words of this prophecy, and blessed are those who hear it and take to heart what is written in it, because the time is near."*

Revelation is the one book in the Bible that says there's a blessing you'll receive if you read it! So, if you need a blessing in your life, take some time to read the book of Revelation as we study what it says and the presence of angels within it.

A Message for the Churches

In the opening chapter of Revelation, John heard a voice like a trumpet that instructed him to write down what he saw—both things in the present and those yet to come—and share the message with the seven churches. When he turns to see who is speaking to him, he sees Jesus with seven stars in His hands, standing in the midst of the seven golden lampstands. Here's the explanation of what John sees in verse 20: "*The seven stars are the angels of the seven churches, and the seven lampstands are the seven churches.*"

Did you know there are angels assigned to churches? I'm quite confident there are angels assigned to our congregation in Murfreesboro, and I believe that's true of other churches, as well. Please don't miss that fact. You see, when we take our places and say we'll do whatever we can to strengthen the Church and add momentum to what God is doing, we join the angels. We join the heavenly host. We're not just filling slots, doing busywork, or meeting religious obligations. We are doing the work of the Kingdom of God.

Beginning in Revelation, chapter 2, there's a message for each of those seven churches, and what is repeated over and over is, "I know what you're about. I know your strengths and your weaknesses. I'm watching."

Jesus is aware of what we're doing and how we're doing our assignments. A deceptive idea that has pervaded our culture is, "What I do in the privacy of my home is my business and nobody else's." I certainly don't want the government involved in the privacy of your home or mine, but God is aware of who we are 24/7. I don't have a "private" Allen and a "public" Allen. I don't have a faith for when I'm standing in front of the congregation and a faith for when I'm in the mall. You don't want to cultivate that notion. You don't want to have a set of ethics for business and a set for church, or a set of ethics for one group of friends and another group of morals for another. The very clear message to those seven churches is that our lives are open before the Lord. Scripture says what we whisper in our bedrooms will be shouted from the housetops.

The seven churches of Revelation were in Asia Minor, which is modern-day Turkey. Before John came to the end of his life, the gospel made it all the way to Rome and around the Mediterranean. But these messages were sent to churches in relatively close proximity to one another.

The Church in Sardis

As I read about the churches, one that feels relevant to me today is the message given to the angel of the church in Sardis. Revelation, chapter 3, verse 1 says, *"To the angel of the church in Sardis write: These are the words of him who holds the seven spirits of God and the seven stars. I know your deeds; you have a reputation of being alive, but you are dead."*

John is telling the church that their reputation is not accurate.

People looked at the church from a secular perspective, and it seemed to be vibrant, vital, and effective—but what about God's perspective?

When we take on a *prophetic perspective*, we see circumstances from the vantage point of God. The prophetic note to the message that's being delivered is, "You have a reputation of being alive, but you're dead."

If you're dead, it would be good to know how to be alive again, and verse 2 says, *"Wake up! Strengthen what remains and is about to die, for I have found your deeds unfinished in the sight of my God."* It's not that their deeds are completely missing; it's that they're incomplete. This is similar to what happened with the church in Galatia, when Paul wrote in Galatians, chapter 5, "What happened to you? You were running a good race, and somebody broke in on you. You've lost all your momentum!" Again, I think we have been trained to focus on our entry point into the Kingdom of God, and then we just wait around and hope we don't make any really big mistakes. But we are called to pursue something more.

There are some characteristics to note about the church of Sardis. It's a church that made the Book, so they were not reprobate; they were asleep. Now, sleep is a normal part of the cycle of life. Sleep is necessary. Without sleep you'll self-destruct. But Proverbs says it's the shameful son who sleeps during harvest. There's a time to be asleep and a time to be awake. When you're asleep, you're unaware, uninvolved, and unconcerned. You're not evil; you just don't care.

Here's a good prayer to ask God to awaken you:

Lord, show me the things I'm unconcerned about or unaware of that I need to see from Your perspective. In Jesus' name, amen.

Do you have the courage to pray that? Are you willing to ask the Spirit of God to give you an assignment, a new direction, an intercessory role?

The church in Sardis was caught asleep and was told, "You're weak. Strengthen what remains and is about to die." If you are in a weakened condition, there are some truths that come along with regaining strength. Awakening brings a heightened awareness that often leads to work. You probably won't be fully prepared for what's been revealed to you, so you'll need to be ready to read, learn, pray, and grow spiritually.

It seems accurate to say the church in Sardis forfeited some things they used to have—and so have we. A few decades ago, a biblical worldview was far more prevalent in the culture around us than it is today. The moral perspectives that are being celebrated and pushed forward in our schools, universities, the media, and wherever you look right now, would have been unimaginable in the not-very-distant past.

We need to remember what we had and not yield the field. Let's not put our hands up and say, "Well, that's just how things go." That's not how things go! The Bible is filled with stories of generation, after generation, after generation of God's people drifting into immoral, ungodly, inappropriate places, and through the repentance of people, God brings them back. God is worthy of our very best efforts, everywhere He leads us.

Guarding Our Hearts

The second sentence of Revelation, chapter 3, verse 4, leapt off the page as I read it: *"They will walk with me, dressed in white, for they are worthy."*

I walked around for several days with the notion of walking worthy of the Lord. Are we walking worthy of the Lord? I'm not talking about avoiding gross immorality or not stealing, but in the momentum of your life and the desires of your heart, are you walking worthy of the Lord? Are we asking Him, "Lord, what would it look like for me to walk in a way that reflects a greater desire to honor You?"

To do this, we need to be careful to guard our hearts. When Jesus addresses the church of Philadelphia in Revelation, chapter 3, verse 11, He says, *"I am coming soon. Hold on to what you have, so that no one will take your crown."* The verse implies a bit of a tug of war; hold on to what you have. There is an attempt to snatch it, diminish it—to take it from you and distract you. That should encourage us to hold on.

Don't give up, and don't give in! Remember, even if you can't see them, the angels are helping you in this battle! Don't yield your thoughts or your emotions to the enemy. Instead, determine to be filled with the joy of the Lord, to honor Him, to celebrate His goodness in the land of the living. He has kept us! We have food, clothing, shelter, and we can worship. He has been good to us!

Let the joy of the Lord begin to seep into your heart, and hold on to what you have!

Angels Are Not All the Same

As we move to Revelation, chapter 5, we see the angels reveal a sealed scroll. Before there were books, long messages were written on scrolls, and they were rolled up and sealed so one could know they hadn't been tampered with or altered. Verses 1 and 2 say, *"Then I saw in the right hand of him who sat on the throne a scroll with writing on both sides and sealed with seven seals. And I saw a mighty angel proclaiming in a loud voice, 'Who is worthy to break the seals and open the scroll?'"*

It's worth noting that the *New International Version* says, *"I saw a mighty angel,"* while the *New American Standard Bible* says, *"I saw a strong angel."* One of the things I want to draw your attention to, as you go through Revelation, is that all angels aren't the same. They have different realms of authority. Some are presented as mighty angels that are uniquely strong. Some have specific assignments.

One of the things I have observed is when you have little

knowledge of something, you assume whatever it is, they're all the same. For instance, many of my Jewish friends have had very little experience with Christians. They think all Christians are the same, and they're quite perplexed when you try to explain there's enormous diversity in how Christians approach the practice of their faith. They know that Hitler was a baptized Catholic, so from their vantage point the Christians created the Holocaust. We're quick to say, "No, no, no. That was not us!"

On the other side of the equation, the general population in America thinks the Jewish people are homogenous. In reality, there's as much diversity in how the Jewish people practice their faith as there is among Christians. Some wear black hats, long sideburns, and long black coats. Others are more lax in the way they give adherence to Scripture. There's a great deal of diversity.

This also applies to topics beyond religion and faith. If you've never been around a horse, you think all horses are the same: They have four legs, a tail, and they snort. If you're a horse person, you know there are tremendous differences. So, whatever you know about, you understand the uniqueness and the differentiation. But what you know little about, you just lump in and think, *They're all the same.*

Well, we've thought all angels were alike, but that's not what Scripture tells us. As a part of this revelation, John sees lots of angels—thousands of them—and as we move forward in our study, you'll recognize they are not all the same.

Who Is Worthy?

The overall theme of Revelation, chapter 5, is worthiness. "Who is worthy?" is the dominant question in this chapter. We just talked earlier in this chapter about walking worthy of the Lord, and I want to understand that better. Revelation, chapter 5, verse 3 says, *"But no one in heaven or on earth or under the earth could open the scroll or even look inside it."*

Righteousness is a gift, but there's a difference in receiving the gift of righteousness (the redemptive work of Jesus and the provision that assures our entrance into the Kingdom of God) and choosing to lead a life worthy of the Lord. Our interest has been so small, our concern has been so little, our awareness has been so minute, that we just dumped it all into the same bucket and said, "Since we accepted Jesus as our Lord and Savior, we're worthy." But Scripture very clearly says that there was *no one* found worthy to open this scroll.

John begins to weep in verses 4 and 5: *"I wept and wept because no one was found who was worthy to open the scroll or look inside. Then one of the elders said to me, 'Do not weep! See, the Lion of the tribe of Judah, the Root of David, has triumphed. He is able to open the scroll and its seven seals.'"*

If you don't take anything else away from this book, remember this—and it needs to be personal: Jesus is worthy.

He is worthy of your service.

He's worthy of your allegiance.

He's worthy of your trust.

He's worthy of your worship.

He is worthy.

We may be talking a lot about angels—their power and authority and help in times of need—but let me remind you that it's Jesus alone who is more worthy than any other being in Heaven, on Earth, or under the earth. Philippians, chapter 2 told us that because of what Jesus did, God gave Him a name that's above every name in Heaven, in the earth, and under the earth. Again, the book of Revelation is not new. It reiterates what we've been told throughout Scripture.

Then, John turned to see the Lion of the Tribe of Judah:

> *Then I saw a Lamb, looking as if it had been slain, standing at the center of the throne, encircled by the four living creatures and the elders. The Lamb had seven horns and seven eyes, which are the seven spirits of God sent out into all the earth. He went and took the scroll from the right hand of Him who sat on the throne. And when He had taken it, the four living creatures and the twenty-four elders fell down before the Lamb. Each one had a harp and they were holding golden bowls full of incense, which are the prayers of God's people. And they sang a new song, saying:*

"You are worthy to take the scroll and to open its seals, because you were slain, and with your blood you purchased for God persons from every tribe and language and people and nation."

REVELATION 5:6-9

Imagine what would have happened if Jesus—the sinless, perfect, obedient, incarnate Son of God—had gotten to Gethsemane and said, "No, I'm just tired. That's too much. It's a bridge too far." In Scripture, we see He struggled with it. In Luke, chapter 22, He said, "If there's any other way, I'd rather go that way." But He submitted Himself to God's will.

Now, I want to ask if you're willing to follow the Lord beyond the acknowledgement of your salvation. I'm grateful you're saved and born again. I'm not suggesting you earn your way into Heaven, but we need to move away from the idea that we have no purpose for our lives other than self-fulfillment.

Revelation, chapter 5, verse 10 talks about our assignment: *"You have made them to be a kingdom and priests to serve our God, and they will reign on the Earth."* Some of you think you're just getting ready to go to Heaven. That's important, but Jesus is coming back to Earth, and we're going to rule and reign with Him *here*! It's time to prepare.

John continues to describe his vision:

Then I looked and heard the voice of many angels, numbering thousands upon thousands, and ten thousand times ten thousand. They encircled the throne and the living creatures and the elders. In a loud voice they were saying: "Worthy is the Lamb, who was slain, to receive power and wealth and wisdom and strength and honor and glory and praise!" Then I heard every creature in heaven and on earth and under the earth and on the sea, and all that is in them, saying: "To Him who sits on the throne and to the Lamb be praise and honor and glory and power, for ever and ever!"

REVELATION 5:11-13

This reflects what Paul says in his letter to the Philippians:

Therefore God exalted him to the highest place and gave him the name that is above every name, that at the name of Jesus every knee should bow, in heaven and on earth and under the earth, and every tongue acknowledge that Jesus Christ is Lord, to the glory of God the Father.

PHILIPPIANS 2:9-11

Again, Revelation is not news. It's just a graphic presentation of what we had been told already: Jesus is worthy. The angels and all the heavenly creatures declare He's worthy of worship, but we are often reluctant worshipers. We'll say, "That's not my style. That's not my favorite leader. I'm not emotional. I'm a bit more introverted." And that's true; some of us are. For some of us, a smile is a tremendous burst of enthusiasm; others of you have a bit more energy. I'm not asking you to choose a new personality, but I am asking you to be genuine in giving glory and honor to the Lord. He is worthy!

The great contest at the End of the Age, the great line of division, the point of demarcation will be: What are you worshiping?

If you don't think Jesus is worthy, did you notice the list of things it says He received: power, wealth, wisdom, strength, honor, glory, and praise? That's a pretty interesting list to me! There are seven things listed there, and they're very similar to what the secular world pursues: power, wealth, wisdom, and the praise of other people. Those things aren't evil, but if you're seeking them instead of putting Jesus in first place, they become idols. Jesus gained each of those things by yielding His life, not by asserting His rights. It's counter intuitive, but so important to understand—our faith often contradicts what culture teaches us.

It feels appropriate to conclude this chapter by offering a proclamation that echoes the angels' declaration in Revelation, chapter 5, verses 12 and 13. Read this aloud:

Worthy is the Lamb, who was slain, to receive power, and wealth, and wisdom, and strength, and honor, and glory, and praise! To Him who sits on the throne and to the Lamb be praise, and honor, and glory, and power, for ever and ever!

06 CHAPTER SIX

THE ANGELS WITH THE SCROLLS

As I said, we're not going to complete the End of the Age without the significant involvement of the angels. So, you'll want to get to know them! If you don't believe they exist, it will be awkward when you see them and you find yourself saying, "Oh, I never believed in you."

In the last chapter, we talked about how John heard the voices of thousands of angels. They were worshiping as the Lamb (Jesus) took the scroll to open the seals. As we begin Revelation, chapter 6, we find the Lamb opening the first of the seven seals on that scroll. It's worth noting that the Lamb will be the One to open every one of those seals.

What's going to happen in the earth at the End of the Age will come as a direct result of Jesus' involvement.

The Four Horsemen

The first seals Jesus opens will reveal the four horsemen of the apocalypse: the white horse, the red horse, the black horse, and the pale horse.

Let's look at the white horse, which we see in Revelation, chapter 6, verses 1 and 2: *"I watched as the Lamb opened the first of the seven seals. Then I heard one of the four living creatures say in a voice like thunder, 'Come!' I looked, and there before me was a white horse! Its rider held a bow, and he was given a crown, and he rode out as a conqueror bent on conquest."*

This was written in the historical context of the Roman Empire, and the Roman emperor rode a white horse and wore a laurel wreath. The laurel wreath was the symbol of a victor—like a gold medal in the Olympics. So, the Roman emperor rode the white horse as a symbol of honor and his position of power, and he wore the decoration of the victor.

You can disagree with me, because it's not explained in perfect detail, but the way I understand the passage is that the white horse is the gospel of Jesus Christ. It's going to ride into the earth, and at the End of the Age we will see the gospel go around the world in an unprecedented way. There will be people gathered from every nation, language, and tribe. The white horse must stay ahead of the other three, because the other three are a bit more threatening.

In verses 3 and 4, the Lamb opens the second seal: *"I heard the second living creature say, 'Come!' Then another horse came out, a fiery red one. Its rider was given power to take peace from the earth and to make people kill each other. To him was given a large sword."*

Again, Jesus is unleashing these things.

As I understand the red horse, it represents conflict. Specifically, ethnic conflict, according to Matthew, chapter 24. When the scripture says, *"nation will rise against nation,"* the Greek word in that passage is *ethnos*, from which we get "ethnic." It's not an overstatement to say ethnic conflict is increasing in the world, and hatred and war will proliferate from that. It's deception to say human beings working together, without regeneration from the Spirit of God, bring peace and harmony. There is no evidence to support that from human history. The current dialogue around socialism, and how we should all receive equal things, is one of the most blatant distortions of human history available to us today. Marxism is responsible for 100 million deaths in the last century. It's a very deceptive ideology.

Revelation, chapter 6, verses 5 and 6 say, *"When the Lamb opened the third seal, I heard the third living creature say, 'Come!' I looked, and there before me was a black horse! Its rider was holding a pair of scales in his hand. Then I heard what sounded like a voice among the four living creatures, saying, 'Two pounds of wheat for a day's wages, and six pounds of barley for a day's wages, and do not damage the oil and the wine!'"*

The black horse is a portrayal of shortage and insufficiency; a fundamental lack of what is needed for people to sustain life. There's not going to be enough to feed a family. It will bring desperation. We've had some brief tremors of that. In Tennessee, if it snows in Kentucky, we buy all the bread and milk available to us. Some of you gathered tremendous hoards of toilet paper at the beginning of the COVID pandemic, as if the lack of toilet paper would usher in the apocalypse. If there were true shortages, imagine the panic it would bring.

Typically in Scripture, oil and wine portray the wealthy, so there seems to be a suggestion that the wealthy are going to be less impacted by this.

We come to the fourth seal in verses 7 and 8: *"I heard a voice of the fourth living creature say, 'Come!' I looked, and there before me was a pale horse! Its rider was named Death, and Hades was following close behind him. They were given power over a fourth of the earth to kill by sword, famine and plague, and by the wild beasts of the earth."*

The pale horse brings death to a fourth of the world's population by sword, famine, plague, and beasts of the earth. That is a pandemic. Death claims the bodies of men, and Hades claims the souls. It's an intimidating passage.

The Wrath of the Lamb

In verse 12, the sixth seal is opened, and the story continues:

> *Then the kings of the earth, the princes, the generals, the rich, the mighty, and everyone else, both slave and free, hid in caves and among the rocks of the mountains. They called to the mountains and the rocks, "Fall on us and hide us from the face of him who sits on the throne and from the wrath of the Lamb! For the great day of their wrath has come, and who can withstand it?"*
>
> REVELATION 6:15-17

Have you ever heard somebody say that Jesus is all about love, or that Jesus is only about love? It's true that God is love, but that's not the whole truth. In this chapter of Revelation, we see the Lamb angered by the condition of the hearts of human beings and unleashing His wrath in the earth. In 2 Timothy, chapter 3, Paul describes fifteen attributes of character of people who have a facade of religious activity. This includes being lovers of money, lovers of pleasure more than lovers of God, and lovers of self. These people will draw the wrath of the Lamb when the sixth seal is opened.

Angels Come into Action

Revelation, chapter 7, starts with four powerful angels who have the power to impact the weather on the planet. Verse 1 says, *"I saw four angels standing at the four corners of the earth, holding back the four winds of the earth to prevent any wind from blowing on the land or on the sea or on any tree."* Once again, we see that angels are significant!

In the same chapter, verses 11 and 12 say, *"All the angels were standing around the throne and around the elders and the four living creatures. They fell down on their faces before the throne and worshiped God, saying: 'Amen! Praise and glory and wisdom and thanks and honor and power and strength be to our God for ever and ever. Amen!'"*

Angels have access to the throne of God, and they are involved in worship. We are given those same permissions in Hebrews, chapter 4, verse 16, which says we can come boldly before the throne of grace to find mercy to help us in our time of need. That's good news! But instead of being excited by this opportunity, we tend to say, "Well, I don't pray much. I'm not much of a pray-er. I don't feel the need to read my Bible—I know the stories." I'm not casting stones or trying to make you feel guilty. I want you to understand the amazing privilege that has been given to us. Worshiping the Lord is a privilege! Approaching the throne of grace is a tremendous honor! It's not a burden—it's the place that will secure our futures. It's the place that will secure our health, our strength, our peace, and the resources we will need when shortages ravage the earth.

When we get to Revelation, chapter 8, we again see the significant role of the angels:

> *When he opened the seventh seal, there was silence in heaven for about half an hour. And I saw the seven angels who stand before God, and seven trumpets were given to them. Another angel, who had a golden censer, came and stood at the altar. He was given much incense to offer, with the prayers of all God's people, on the golden altar in front of the throne.*
>
> REVELATION 8:1-3

Then, verse 7 says, "*The first angel sounded his trumpet, and there came hail and fire mixed with blood, and it was hurled down on the earth. A third of the earth was burned up, a third of the trees were burned up, and all the green grass was burned up.*" This was a powerful angel entrusted with a very significant assignment.

We're introduced to more angels as the story continues:

> *The sixth angel sounded his trumpet, and I heard a voice coming from the four horns of the golden altar that is before God. It said to the sixth angel who had the trumpet, "Release the four angels who are bound at the great river Euphrates." And the four angels who had been kept ready for this very hour and day and month and year were released to kill a third of mankind.*
>
> REVELATION 9:13-15

These angels have been waiting for that exact moment in time, and they have the ability and assignment to kill a third of mankind. Angels are powerful spiritual beings.

The COVID virus made an impact on the earth, but not of the magnitude of what this scripture talks about. We believe in that virus, even though we can't see it, and appropriately so. We changed behaviors, habits, and patterns. Almost every aspect of our lives was affected by it. But we'll have debates about whether or not we believe in spiritual beings and their influence upon us. We'll point to the fact that we've been born again, or converted, or saved—so talking about it more is not necessary. It's insignificant. That's a very childish imagination of the Kingdom of God. We have much more information available to us than that, and we need to be informed.

Many Forms of Debauchery

Even though these terrible things will come to pass, it won't stop the debauchery of the people left on Earth. Revelation, chapter 9, verse 20 says, *"The rest of mankind who were not killed by these plagues still did not repent of the work of their hands; they did not stop worshiping demons, and idols of gold, silver, bronze, stone and wood—idols that cannot see or hear or walk."*

When it says *idols*, we tend to think of little statues, and we need to reposition that imagination a little bit. The accumulation of gold and silver is very clearly an idol. We'll compromise our character and do almost anything to accumulate material possessions.

Similarly, when it talks about wood and stone, don't just think of images shaped out of wood and stone. Think about what we build with wood and stone. Where will you cut a corner or compromise your integrity to gain something built out of wood and stone that's a little larger than your current version? Those attitudes are still very prevalent these days.

Verse 21 continues, *"Nor did they repent of their murders, their magic arts, their sexual immorality or their thefts."* Magic arts, the occult, and the pursuit of spiritual influences apart from the Holy Spirit, includes everything from reading a horoscope to practicing yoga. Many Christians are offended by these practices, but do we sincerely understand how to separate ourselves from them and their spiritual influences? Are we willing to use our voices to help others avoid them as well?

What This Means for Us

As we look at the many ways people will fall away from God even after the four horsemen and the plagues, here is the contrast I would like you to notice: In the midst of all of this supernatural activity, there are still an almost innumerable number of angels who are worshiping God. The prayers of God's people are being offered on the altar before the Lord, and there's tremendous spiritual activity taking place.

The white horse of the gospel, ridden out into the whole Earth, has to stay ahead of the red horse, the black horse, and the pale horse. Yet a significant portion of humanity will be recalcitrant, unapologetic, and determined in their ungodliness. In the midst of judgment, they will refuse to repent. They'll continue in murder, the occult, their sexual immorality, and their greed.

I think it's very relevant to where we are. God began to shake the earth in 2020 when businesses, schools, and churches were closed, and holiday and travel plans were interrupted. Our well-being and our physical health were threatened. It sounds like a tremor, a foreshadowing of some of the things that we read in the book of Revelation, doesn't it?

Out of that shaking came the beginning of an awakening. People began to repent. We baptized thousands of people from our church, our community, and even from across the nation—and more are still coming! We baptized a man who brought his family from Long Island, New York. They drove to Tennessee because he wanted his grandson to see him being baptized. I'm grateful for that! But alongside this spiritual awakening, we also see an increased number of people who are unapologetic and unrepentant about rejecting God.

Remember Nineveh

In my opinion, we're not quite to the End of the Age. In fact, that's an understatement. I think we have a way to go. The model we want to think about is Nineveh. Jonah walked through the city for four days and said, "In forty days, God is going to destroy you." In Jonah's heart, he hoped God would do exactly that. He had no compassion. He didn't want to go to Nineveh in the first place. He finally went because God told him to go, and it was better than drowning!

After Jonah delivered his message, he sat down on a hill to watch destruction come, but something unique began to happen in Nineveh. The inhabitants of the city—from the most powerful to the most humble—chose to repent and to humble themselves before God. They even involved their livestock in fasting. And God relented.

I haven't seen a Nineveh response to our current situation yet. But I do see a response beginning, and people are hungrier for truth than I've ever experienced before. I find tremendous hope in that.

Think of the difference between Nineveh and Sodom, where God said, "If I can find ten righteous people, I'll spare the city." God didn't, and Sodom was burned to ash (see Genesis 19:24).

Think of the difference between Nineveh and Noah's day. Noah was a preacher of righteousness, and for all the years he was building the ark, he was preaching to the people, but they didn't care. Only Noah and his family survived the great flood.

Think of Jesus in Jerusalem and the apostles. After Jesus ascended to Heaven, there was a stirring in the city, and the public officials called the apostles in to tell them, "If you don't stop this, we'll kill you, too." Many were martyred, but the threat of death didn't stop them from fulfilling the assignments God gave them.

As we move forward in time, we're getting a little closer to the book of Revelation, and the tension between truth and deception grows. To cultivate the discernment we need, we have to have a heart change. You and me. But what does that look like?

I think we start with those little, quiet prayers I've been inviting you toward, like this:

Lord, if there's anything keeping me from Your best plans for me, open my eyes. I want to walk worthy of You. Lord, give me eyes to see You. Let me be more aware of spiritual things. In Jesus' name, amen.

As an aside, let me just say you don't have to be weird to be spiritual. Weird does not make you spiritual. If you're out of gas, you don't need a word from the Lord—you need cash and a gas station! Canceling your insurance does not make you a person of faith. You also don't need to be loud or bizarre. The most remarkably spiritual people I have ever known—people who experienced miracles as a matter of routine in their lives—were the most normal people I've ever met. Don't imagine you have to amp up your weirdness to be spiritual.

To be honest, I think being weird with your spirituality is an expression of carnality. True spirituality will not draw attention to you; it will draw attention to the Lord. Jesus will be the One who gets the glory and the honor. If the Lord shows you something, unless He tells you to tell it, hush. If He can't trust you to be quiet with the things just meant for you, He may not tell you anything else.

We want to be trustworthy. Walking worthy of the Lord means that He can trust us. Jesus trusted John with that revelation. Can He trust you?

It's an important season in the earth, and you are so important to God's purposes. God knows the worst parts about us, and He's made provision for that—He will use us anyway! He promises to help us—and sometimes that help will come through His angels!

LET'S PRAY

Father, thank You for Your Word and its truth. Thank You for the angels You have sent to serve and minister to Your people. Lord, forgive me for where I've been indifferent or could not have cared less. I've been unaware and asleep. Lord, awaken me. Stir my heart. Let the fear of the Lord come upon me and grow within me. Give me a desire to know You, to worship You, and to seek You beyond anything I've ever known before. I thank You for it. In Jesus' name, amen.

07 CHAPTER SEVEN

ANGELS WITH GREAT AUTHORITY

Most people think the book of Revelation is about Antichrist, the Devil, the False Prophet, and all the wicked things that will happen at the End of the Age. In truth, the overwhelming majority of Revelation is about what God is doing through His angels in the earth. It's an important perspective that takes a lot of the fear out of the book.

As we continue to go through Revelation, remember, my goal isn't to unpack the entire book for you—I'm just trying to call your attention to the activity of the angels and their role in the End of the Age.

Throughout the book, we see many mighty angels at work on

behalf of the people of God. That's not just rhetoric. There are three places specifically in the book of Revelation where it says, "I saw a mighty angel," including Revelation, chapter 10, verse 1: *"Then I saw another mighty angel coming down from heaven. He was robed in a cloud, with a rainbow above his head; his face was like the sun, and his legs were like fiery pillars."*

We've discussed this before, but it's worth reiterating that throughout the Bible we see many types of God-honoring angels—they are not all the same. They have different realms of authority. They have different assignments. They're different in stature. Their appearance suggests some are mightier than others.

We'll continue our study in Revelation with chapter 11, verse 15: *"The seventh angel sounded his trumpet, and there were loud voices in heaven, which said: 'The kingdom of the world has become the kingdom of our Lord and of his Messiah, and he will reign for ever and ever.'"*

Here we see the seventh angel announcing that the kingdom of the world has become the Kingdom of our Lord. We've been praying for this event to take place for as long as we've been Christ-followers. It's part of the Lord's prayer, *"Our Father in heaven, hallowed be your name, your kingdom come, your will be done, on earth as it is in heaven"* (Matthew 6:9-10). Revelation confirms that what we've been praying for all these decades is ahead of us!

But the arrival of God's Kingdom doesn't come without

a conflict. In Revelation, chapter 12, we find a war in the heavenlies, and this is where we tend to become uncomfortable. We'd rather have the purposes of God break forth without any conflict. I appreciate that desire, but I need to tell you it's not scriptural.

I wish summer vegetables would come out of the ground without any effort. I would sit in the house on the sofa and pray my garden into existence. I'm a man of faith and power, but you're smart enough to know that unless I till the ground, sow the seed, pull the weeds, and water the plants, I'm going to be a man of faith and power with no vegetables. There's some effort involved!

Similarly, I assure you that unless we invest the effort in God's Kingdom, we won't see the purposes of God break forth.

The Role of the Archangel Michael

Revelation, chapter 12, verses 7 and 8 say, *"Then war broke out in heaven. Michael and his angels fought against the dragon [Satan], and the dragon and his angels fought back. But he was not strong enough, and they lost their place in heaven."*

The phrase "Michael and his angels" catches my attention because it clearly implicates there's an organizational structure in place; there are realms of authority in the Kingdom of God. In Scripture we find archangels, chief angels, and angels with unique assignments and specific authorities. Michael and Gabriel are two examples. Here we see Michael—and the angels who are under his authority—fighting against the dragon.

The dragon is Satan, and it's good to remember Satan has already been defeated. He was kicked out of Heaven. He lost his place, and a third of the angels left with him. Through the cross, they were completely, eternally, irreversibly defeated. Satan's kingdom was taken from him, but he hasn't quit trying to fight. Verse 9 says, *"The great dragon was hurled down—that ancient serpent called the devil, or Satan, who leads the whole world astray. He was hurled to the earth, and his angels with him."*

Satan isn't creative. He's an imitator. When he was a participant in the Kingdom of God, he saw God's Kingdom and all its glory. He saw its fullness and its structure. So, when he was displaced, he put a similar structure in place in the kingdom he presides over. We'll talk about that a bit more in the chapters ahead.

The Archangel Michael had a very specific assignment, as we see in the book of Daniel. He was sent to Daniel, a Jewish man and a slave in Babylon. Daniel was so revered and honored by God, that God sent angelic messengers to tell him what will happen at the End of the Age. God needed a trustworthy servant to deliver the message, and He found that in Daniel.

It's clear that every generation isn't overly populated with trustworthy servants. That's something we can all aspire to be—a person God can trust to care about His Kingdom, His purposes, and His agenda. Many of us have put disproportional attention on God giving us what we want, thinking that serving the Lord should come secondary to our own wants and desires. Our approach has been illogical and irrational. We reason, "I can make more money doing this," or "I can go do what I'm good at, then pay somebody else to go serve the Lord." That's not how it works.

God is not asking us to quit our jobs—He's asking us to open our hearts to Him in some new ways. We need to make more room in our lives for Him because He's the only One who is going to secure our future. He's the only One who can secure us from the threats around us. He's the only One who will maintain our liberties and our freedoms because so often the rules and regulations that were put in place are set aside. God can do these things, but we have to know Him.

So, back to Daniel, the slave in Babylon. He didn't get to go back to Jerusalem. As far as we know, he was never delivered from that role of slave. Can you imagine being so highly esteemed that God would give you messages about the End of the Age and yet leave you to serve as a slave?

I have been guilty on this point. I've threatened God: "I'm going to withdraw from the team if You don't shape up." Do you ever say anything like that to the Lord? I've shaken my fist and said, "Your job performance is awful, and You better pay a little more attention, or I am looking for an exit!" God can handle our frustrations. Often, the best thing we can do is tell God exactly how we feel. (He already knows, anyway!) Being honest with

God opens the door to receiving His help.

God sent Daniel multiple messages, and in Daniel, chapter 12, verse 1, we find a little more information about Michael. *"At that time Michael, the great prince who protects your people, will arise."* Here, we see that Michael was assigned to watch over the Jewish people.

In the New Testament, Jude offers this insight about Michael in verse 9: *"But even the archangel Michael, when he was disputing with the devil about the body of Moses, did not himself dare to condemn him for slander but said, 'The Lord rebuke you!'"*

The Archangel Michael has protected God's people across history, and He will be protecting them at the End of the Age as well.

Angels Help Us Proclaim the Gospel

We see another angel in Revelation, chapter 14, verse 6. John said, *"Then I saw another angel flying in midair, and he had the eternal gospel to proclaim to those who live on the earth—to every nation, tribe, language and people."* This angel wasn't mighty. He didn't have legs like pillars, but he was flying in mid-air, and he had a big assignment: Proclaim the gospel to those who live on the earth—to every nation, tribe, language, and people.

Have you thought about the fact that there's an angel assigned to see that the gospel is delivered to the whole Earth? Did you know we have spiritual assistants who will help us proclaim the gospel? Hallelujah, we've got some help!

We have a God-given assignment to stand for the gospel—not to just hire others to do it for us. We are the delivery system. Second Corinthians, chapter 5, verse 20 says, *"We are therefore Christ's ambassadors, as though God were making his appeal through us."*

We like to imagine that if God is helping us, then the gate should swing open, and the yellow brick road should flow out in front of us. But what happened to Daniel? He was given an administrative position, and he did so well that his peer group became jealous of him. They manipulated the system so he would be destroyed. That's not the way we want it to work.

It would be the same as if you asked the Lord to help you at work, and He blessed you, and you did so well, your coworkers hated you for it.

Again, sometimes we imagine the blessings of God will be fun, easy, and happy. But we seek the Lord, read our Bibles, pray, fast, and then discover the walk is not easy. Let me remind you of what's in the Book. God said we would encounter hardship, trouble, and opposition. We see just one example of this in the life of David—a man after God's own heart. David's son, Absalom, mobilized the army to try to kill him and did everything in his power to humiliate David in public. Our assignment will come with some adversity. We need God's help—and He might send His ministering angels to do that job.

There's a battle in the earth, and we don't have to go to Washington, D.C. to see it. God has put us in our specific communities for a reason. You have neighbors. Your kids have friends, and they go to schools. In those places, we are called to stand up for God's Truth. We think, *That will be awkward and inconvenient.* Yes, it could be, but it will also change the destiny of children, families, cities, communities, and nations.

The King is coming back! There's an eternity in front of us, and we have a relatively brief period of time to tell our story.

The good news is we have help from Jesus' angels—both now and at the End of the Age!

LET'S PRAY

Thank You for every person praying this prayer, Lord. They are precious in Your sight. There's a purpose for their lives, with a call and anointing upon them, and I thank You for it. Lord, strengthen us. Send the angels to help us. Release Your angels to help deconstruct the barriers and the resistance so we can overcome every attack of the enemy. We thank You for the victory that is ours because the Lamb was slain and His blood was shed, so we might be delivered, justified, and sanctified, with the power of the enemy broken over our lives. Help us be worthy of Your calling and give us the strength and courage to stand, wherever You lead us. In Jesus' name, amen.

08 CHAPTER EIGHT

ANGELS AND JUDGMENT

As we've seen through the last several chapters, angels are very much involved with the judgment at the End of the Age, but most of us haven't paid much attention to their presence. Moving further into Revelation, we see that plagues come to the earth. But these aren't being sponsored by the Devil—God's angels usher them in.

This is shown to us in Revelation, chapter 15, verses 1 and 2: *"I saw in heaven another great and marvelous sign: seven angels with the seven last plagues—last, because with them God's wrath is completed. And I saw what looked like a sea of glass glowing with fire and, standing beside the sea, those who had been victorious over the beast and its image and over the number of its name."*

These seven angels have specific assignments in overseeing God's judgment, and we'll cover only a few of them here.

An Angel in Charge of the Waters

Revelation, chapter 16, verses 4 and 5 say, *"The third angel poured out his bowl on the rivers and springs of water, and they became blood. Then I heard the angel in charge of the waters ...."*

There's an angel in charge of the waters! We've thought so little about it. There are mighty angels, archangels, angels with the gospel, and angels in charge of the waters! Angels oversee God's judgment. Angelic authority plays a significant role in our physical world and the heavenly realm.

An Angel Commissioned to the Sun

We see another mighty angel in Revelation, chapter 16, verses 8 and 9, which say, *"The fourth angel poured out his bowl on the sun, and the sun was allowed to scorch people with fire. They were seared by the intense heat and they cursed the name of God, who had control over these plagues, but they refused to repent and glorify him."*

Please note, God will control the plagues—but the people will refuse to repent and to glorify Him. I know this may be disruptive to your theology, but how God responds to us reflects our response to Him.

An Angel Issues Judgment on the Throne of the Beast

The description of the plagues goes on in verses 10 and 11: *"The fifth angel poured out his bowl on the throne of the beast, and its kingdom was plunged into darkness. People gnawed their tongues in agony and cursed the God of heaven because of their pains and their sores, but they refused to repent of what they had done."*

Here we see two different responses from the angels—two expressions of God's judgment—but the peoples' response is the same. They refuse to repent of what they had done.

A Nineveh Response

In chapter six, we discussed the need for a Nineveh response. The city of Nineveh was given a message from Jonah, a foreigner who didn't like them. He said, "In forty days, God is going to destroy this city." The people responded. From the most powerful person in the city to the least, they repented, and God changed His mind.

We need a Nineveh response in our world today!

At the End of the Age, the reason God's judgments are coming is because people refuse to repent. They refuse to glorify Him. God is not arbitrary. He knows our hearts. Repentance is not some casual thing you do when you feel like it, when you're tired of the ungodliness, or you've pushed it as far as you want to push it. Repentance is the attitude you want to hold when you realize you've taken the slightest step away from God's best in your life. When that happens, you'll want to say, "Lord, I'm sorry, I don't want to do that anymore. I don't want to push that boundary any further. I don't want to justify it or explain it. I don't want to look for a reason. I'm sorry. Please forgive me."

This battle takes place in every generation. It's not a new thing, and it's not something that's just going to happen at the End of the Age. Romans, chapter 1, tells us that every person knows there is a God, but then it describes a downward progression. Verse 21 says, *"For although they knew God, they neither glorified him as God nor gave thanks to him, but their thinking became futile and their foolish hearts were darkened."* This is a very similar description to what Revelation, chapter 16, tells us will take place at the End of the Age.

In Revelation, we see some who are triumphant over the Beast—they celebrate their victory in the name of the Lord. Then there's another group in the midst of God's judgment who are cursing God and refusing to repent. They will not glorify Him. Which category are you going to be in?

We haven't talked about those categories much. We've talked about being saved or not saved, born again or not born again, converted or not converted, baptized or not baptized. Those are all appropriate things. I believe in them. But there's a significant importance in being quick to repent, and we tend to forget that.

An Angel Who Ushers in the End

Revelation, chapter 16, verses 17 and 18 say, *"The seventh angel poured out his bowl into the air, and out of the temple came a loud voice from the throne, saying, 'It is done!' Then there came flashes of lightning, rumblings, peals of thunder and a severe earthquake. No earthquake like it has ever occurred since mankind has been on earth, so tremendous was the quake."*

We've experienced some dramatic earthquakes. Historical photos document earthquake damage that is almost beyond belief. I've visited places around the world where entire cities were destroyed by them, buried in mudslides, and never brought back to life again. Revelation tells us of an angel who ushers in an earthquake that's greater than any the world has ever known.

As I read that, I am reminded of a little verse in the book of Isaiah. I don't know if Isaiah's describing that season in Revelation, but it seems appropriate to me. In Isaiah, chapter 30, verse 25, he describes a day of great slaughter, when "the towers fall." Imagine the cityscapes of the beautiful cities all over the world. There's a day coming when the towers of these cities are going to fall. They will no longer be expressions of power and wealth, or human pride and accomplishment. The Creator of all things will respond to the people who will neither repent nor honor Him.

This all illustrates why we want to lead lives that give glory to the Lord! Whatever we accomplish, we accomplish because of His gifts in our lives, His help, and His opportunities. Our lives are a canvas for His grace.

The Bible says we're fearfully and wonderfully made, and I don't want to denigrate that. I think it's a wonderful thing the Lord has done, creating each of us—but it's for His glory! We serve at His pleasure and for His purposes. This doesn't mean attending unending church services—you have lives, responsibilities, and families. You have life assignments. But in the midst of all of those assignments, glorify the Lord. Let everybody know you follow Jesus.

LET'S PRAY

Heavenly Father, I offer myself as a living sacrifice before You. You have given me life and have delivered me from the kingdom of darkness. Grant me a willing spirit to sustain me. Forgive me of my sins. I choose to forgive those who have sinned against me. Establish me, and I will rest in the security of Your watchful care. I choose to finish the course for which I was created. May You be glorified. In Jesus' name, amen.

09 CHAPTER NINE

ANGELS AND THE END OF THE AGE

We're often afraid of the book of Revelation, but it is not just the story of the destruction of Antichrist, Satan, or the False Prophet. It's the unveiling of the story of God bringing His judgment and His Kingdom into this world through His angels and Jesus. It's a description of a birth, and it's a wonderful story.

For the last several chapters we've been highlighting some of the angels in Revelation—their strength, their power, and the prominent role they play in bringing about the End of the Age. In fact, if I had to give you a summary of those last three chapters, it would be this: Something good is going to happen to you! Begin to approach Revelation with this perspective, and it will change how you understand the book.

The first few chapters in Revelation deal with John's present time and the seven churches he knew in Asia Minor. The middle section discusses the season ahead of John. The last couple of chapters concern the distant future, the ultimate judgment, and the establishment of Christ reigning on Earth. (John saw that vision 2,000 years ago, so that distant future has become a lot shorter!) In this chapter, we will discuss the angels and some other insight from the last section of Revelation.

An Illuminated Angel

Revelation, chapter 18, verse 1 says, *"I saw another angel coming down from heaven. He had great authority, and the earth was illuminated by his splendor."* By this point, John had seen millions of angels, but this one was different—it had great authority, and the splendor of his presence lit up the earth. Do you have an imagination of angels like that? Do you still think all angels are the same?

An Angel Who Will Bind Satan

Revelation, chapter 20, verses 1 and 2 say, *"And I saw an angel coming down out of heaven, having the key to the Abyss and holding in his hand a great chain. He seized the dragon, that ancient serpent, who is the devil, or Satan, and bound him for a thousand years."*

Here we see a single angel who has God's authority to bind Satan and throw him into the Abyss. This is the moment we have all been waiting for! The revelation continues in verse 3: *"He threw him into the Abyss, and locked and sealed it over him, to keep him from deceiving the nations anymore until the thousand years were ended. After that, he must be set free for a short time."*

A New Beginning

Then, in Revelation, chapter 21, verse 1, we see a new beginning: *"Then I saw 'a new heaven and a new earth,' for the first heaven and the first earth had passed away, and there was no longer any sea."*

Though this sounds glorious, new beginnings often feel difficult. Humans don't like change, even when they are good changes. We like home cooking. We like our favorite pair of blue jeans. We like the way we've always done it.

It makes me think of when churches grow and need to expand, but there's hesitation about taking steps forward to accommodate new people. It's almost as if our attitude is, "Well, I found my space. Let them go find their own." We understand, intuitively, that change means we can't maintain our routines, and there could be some new things asked of us.

So, when we read about a new Heaven and a new Earth, I think there is something subconscious that says, "I'm not sure this is good. I might be against this. Is there going to be fried chicken in the new Heaven and the new Earth?"

We gain more insight as we continue to read:

> *I saw the Holy City, the new Jerusalem, coming down out of heaven from God, prepared as a bride beautifully dressed for her husband. And I heard a loud voice from the throne*

saying, "Look! God's dwelling place is now among the people, and he will dwell with them. They will be his people, and God himself will be with them and be their God. 'He will wipe every tear from their eyes. There will be no more death' or mourning or crying or pain, for the old order of things has passed away."

REVELATION 21:2-4

I'm thinking this sounds like an upgrade! Something good is going to happen to you!

The good news continues in verses 5 and 6: *"He who was seated on the throne said, 'I am making everything new!' Then he said, 'Write this down, for these words are trustworthy and true.' He said to me: 'It is done. I am the Alpha and the Omega, the Beginning and the End. To the thirsty I will give water without cost from the spring of the water of life.'"*

Blessings for Those Who Overcome

How will we get to experience this new Heaven and Earth? What do we need to do? We find relevant information in Revelation, chapter 21, verse 7: *"'He who overcomes shall inherit all things, and I will be his God and he shall be My son'"* (NKJV®).

When Revelation talks about the seven churches that each get a message, it says, "They will have to overcome." The book is written to the broader Church—Church with a capital "C"—and when we get to the triumphant chapters of the establishment of the Kingdom of God on Earth, it says, "The one who will inherit many blessings is the one who overcomes." God is calling us to be overcomers! Overcoming pre-supposes obstacles, difficulties, hurdles, inconveniences, and unwanted things. That is what's ahead of us, but we need to remember that there are blessings as we endure.

What's the opposite of being an overcomer? I can think of many bad character traits, including cowardice. Verse 8 says, *"But the cowardly, the unbelieving, the vile, the murderers, the sexually immoral, those who practice magic arts, the idolators and all liars—they will be consigned to the fiery lake of burning sulfur. This is the second death."* Cowardice is choosing not to confront, not to stand, or to compromise the truth. There is always a reason for it or a way to justify it. We'll push our logic through whatever formula is necessary to gain the outcomes we prefer.

It takes courage to follow the Lord. It takes determination to take the truth of God and say, "I will own that for myself." It begins with a personal decision. If we're not willing to demonstrate the courage it takes to choose the truth for ourselves, we won't be able to stand. We won't be able to overcome. We may still sit in churches. We may sing the songs and carry our Bibles. We may even read Bibles, lead groups, and do all sorts of things, but destructive behaviors will begin to creep into our lives if we aren't actively engaged in fighting them—and that takes a personal commitment to the Truth.

Knowing When to Stand

Our challenge is to be led by the Spirit of God so we understand when we're supposed to stand for Him and His truth, and when we should remain still and trust. We don't always stand in defiance. Sometimes God fights the battle for us and leads us through a narrow hedge of safety, and our job is to simply follow.

When the angels released Peter from prison in Acts, chapter 12, he was slated for execution. He had been in prison for several days, and God sent an angelic contingent to unlock his chains, silence the soldiers around him, and open the prison doors before him. Peter didn't open the doors. They were opened for him by an angel.

After Peter escaped the prison, he went and found the believers at an all-night prayer meeting. He knocked on the door when he arrived, and it took a little while for them to let him in—they didn't believe it was actually him! Isn't it good to know we're with that crew? Are you ever surprised when God moves? I am, too!

What Peter said to them is what always captures my emotion: "Tell James and the other brothers and sisters I came to see you." Then, he left for another place. He didn't linger with his friends. There were multiple occasions in the book of Acts when they were delivered from a threat, and the angels told them, "Go back to the Temple Mount. Finish the sermon they interrupted." But not that day—Peter was told to leave. So, when I say we're called to stand, we need God's wisdom on when to do that, what it looks like, and how He would like us to do so.

Blessings Ahead

We get a glimpse of the blessings that come from overcoming in Revelation, chapter 22, verses 1 and 2, which say: *"Then the angel showed me the river of the water of life, as clear as crystal, flowing from the throne of God and of the Lamb down the middle of the great street of the city."* You'll see that place one day!

The glorious vision continues:

> *On each side of the river stood the tree of life, bearing twelve crops of fruit, yielding its fruit every month. And the leaves of the tree are for the healing of the nations. No longer will there be any curse. The throne of God and of the Lamb will be in the city, and his servants will serve him. They will see his face, and his name will be on their foreheads. There will be no more night. They will not need the light of a lamp or the light of the sun, for the Lord God will give them light. And they will reign for ever and ever. The angel said to me, "These words are trustworthy and true. The Lord, the God who inspires the prophets, sent his angel to show his servants the things that must soon take place."*
>
> REVELATION 22:2-6

We see John's response in verse 8: *"I, John, am the one who heard and saw these things. And when I had heard and seen them, I fell down to worship at the feet of the angel who had been showing them to me."*

What an amazing journey. What amazing insight he had been given! He saw the throne of Heaven. He saw 100 million angels—that's about a third of the current population of the United States! He saw what was to come in the future. He responded by falling at the feet of the one who had been guiding him through this revelation, but in verse 9 the angel tells him, *"'Don't do that! I am a fellow servant with you and with your fellow prophets and with all who keep the words of this scroll. Worship God!'"*

I want you to hear that truth for just a moment so it finds a new place in your heart: There are angels serving *with* you. Do you ever feel alone? Maybe you hear the news, or you hear people in powerful positions mocking God, or you see expressions of evil that seem to be supported by enormous resources, or all sorts of stuff—whatever it is that makes you feel isolated and alone. I find tremendous comfort and real courage from reading that one little insight from the angel who said, "I am a fellow servant with you." There are angels serving with me, and they are serving with you, too.

Look at the clarity, understanding, and insight the angel had. He says it so clearly, so succinctly, so plainly, and so directly—and yet every one of us, in an honest moment, would have to confess that we've debated every point in that sentence. We've thought,

Is there really a God? Were the prophets real or just kooks? Is the Bible actually God's Word?

The angel has such clarity, and the outcome he leads us to is this: "Worship God!"

LET'S PRAY

Heavenly Father, thank You for Your Word. Thank You that You're still searching the earth for men and women who have a heart toward You. Lord, we turn our hearts to receive all You have for us. Give us understanding hearts. Give us a vision beyond ourselves. Father, thank You that You've called us to this unique season, and that in new ways, we will see Your Kingdom come and Your will be done, on Earth as it is in Heaven. In Jesus' name, amen.

10 CHAPTER TEN

ANGELS IN ZECHARIAH

Revelation isn't just a story about the End of the Age. It's also not full of brand-new ideas—many of its themes echo those previously presented in the Bible, and the Old Testament book of Zechariah provides a great example of this. What we see the angels doing in Zechariah is a forerunner to what we find in the book of Revelation.

The book of Zechariah begins with a vision and an angelic visitor:

> *During the night I had a vision, and there before me was a man mounted on a red horse. He was standing among the myrtle trees in a ravine. Behind him were red, brown and white horses. I asked, "What are these, my lord?" The*

angel who was talking with me answered, "I will show you what they are." Then the man standing among the myrtle trees explained, "They are the ones the LORD has sent to go throughout the earth."

ZECHARIAH 1:8-10

This description sounds a lot like the four horsemen in Revelation, chapter 6, doesn't it? Remember discussing the white horse of the gospel, the red horse, the black horse, and the pale horse? What John described in the book of Revelation was easy for him to put into words because he was familiar with the book of Zechariah. He understood he was placed in a heritage of people whose faith was described, defined, and made possible by the interaction of angels on their journey.

I suspect we have more confidence in our affiliation with a denomination, a congregation, or a translation of the Bible than we do in our relationship with angels. I've spent my life in the Church. I'm not opposed to any of those things, but angels occupy an important part of our journey. They're fellow servants who are here to help us. It's worthwhile to become familiar with them!

A Vision of an Angel with Joshua

Zechariah, chapter 3, verses 1 and 2 say, *"Then he showed me Joshua the high priest standing before the angel of the LORD, and Satan standing at his right side to accuse him. The LORD said to*

Satan, 'The LORD rebuke you, Satan! The LORD, who has chosen Jerusalem, rebuke you!'"

This seems like a good place to mention that the Hebrew word for *Satan* means "accuser"—so, what would the accuser do? Accuse Joshua, the High Priest of Israel—even as he was standing in the presence of an angel. The story continues:

> *"Is not this man a burning stick snatched from the fire?" Now Joshua was dressed in filthy clothes as he stood before the angel. The angel said to those who were standing before him, "Take off his filthy clothes." Then he said to Joshua, "See, I have taken away your sin, and I will put fine garments on you." Then I said, "Put a clean turban on his head." So they put a clean turban on his head and clothed him, while the angel of the LORD stood by. The angel of the LORD gave this charge to Joshua: "This is what the LORD Almighty says: 'If you will walk in obedience to me and keep my requirements, then you will govern my house and have charge of my courts, and I will give you a place among these standing here.'"*
>
> ZECHARIAH 3:2-7

This passage provides a very graphic portrayal of what God has done for you and me. He's taken away our sin. We've been given a robe of righteousness that we didn't earn, didn't deserve, and certainly couldn't purchase. How we respond shows how much we value this gift. If you live a shabby, sloppy life, dishonoring God, you don't attach much value to the gift. On the other hand, we don't choose to honor the Lord with our lives, our emotions, our words, or our behaviors so God will love us more—He loved us when we were committed pagans. A righteous life is how we express appreciation and gratitude—and demonstrate the value we attach to that gift.

Thinking about this graphic portrayal of Joshua's filthy clothing being replaced with clean ones leads me back to the pictures of Revelation and the message to the church in Laodicea—which is also a message to the Church today.

Revelation, chapter 3, verses 17 and 18 say, *"You say, 'I am rich; I have acquired wealth and do not need a thing.' But you do not realize that you are wretched, pitiful, poor, blind and naked. I counsel you to buy from me gold refined in the fire, so you can become rich; and white clothes to wear, so you can cover your shameful nakedness; and salve to put on your eyes, so you can see."*

The church in Laodicea had been given the gift of righteousness and said they had all they needed—but the outcome of their lives resulted in them being blind, pitiful, naked, and in need of all things. Does that description sound familiar? We have so many resources physically, yet we walk around spiritually blind, pitiful, naked, and in need. We are going to need spiritual help to wake out of the slumber we've been in.

An Angel Awakens Zechariah

Zechariah offers a helpful passage in Zechariah, chapter 4, verse 1, which says, "*Then the angel who talked with me returned and woke me up, like someone awakened from sleep.*"

We all have some friends who are still a bit asleep spiritually. They may be good people—people of faith, or people with a heritage of faith—but they're still a bit asleep. They're not awake to what God is doing. Don't be angry with them—they need God's help. Begin to quietly say, "Thank You, Lord, for the way You are waking me up. Show me any areas where I'm still asleep, and wake up the people around me. Awaken Your people, Lord. Send an angel, if necessary. Stir our hearts by Your Spirit, Lord."

The angelic interaction in the book of Zechariah continues:

> *He asked me, "What do you see?" I answered, "I see a solid gold lampstand with a bowl at the top and seven lamps on it, with seven channels to the lamps. Also there are two olive trees by it, one on the right of the bowl and the other on its left." I asked the angel who talked with me, "What are these, my lord?" He answered, "Do you not know what these are?" "No, my lord," I replied. So he said to me, "This is the word of the LORD to Zerubbabel: 'Not by might nor by power, but by my Spirit,' says the LORD Almighty.'"*
>
> ZECHARIAH 4:2-6

Do you know who Zerubbabel is? Do you happen to know the contribution he made to Jewish history? I'll give you a hint: Solomon built the First Temple in Jerusalem, and it was destroyed by the Babylonians in 587 B.C. The Second Temple was built in Jerusalem under the authority of a Persian king. The Jews had not all returned from exile yet, but they had been given permission to rebuild that Second Temple in Jerusalem—and Zerubbabel, from the lineage of King David, was the one who built it. To this day, the Jewish people understand their history in terms of the First Temple period and the Second Temple period.

The Second Temple was a very modest building—they didn't have the wealth Solomon had available when he built the first one. Their resources were few, they were still slaves in a foreign land, and though the exiles had begun to return, there were not great numbers of them. The encouragement the angel brought to Zerubbabel was, *"'Not by might nor by power, but by my Spirit,' says the LORD Almighty."*

When Solomon built the Temple, it was one of the most beautiful buildings ever constructed. Zerubbabel was not going to rival that, but he had been given an assignment, and God said, "Zerubbabel, you can accomplish this. But it won't be by your physical might, or the power of the numbers that you marshal. It will be by the Spirit of the Living God."

I believe that if there was a message for the Church in the world today, it would be, "Not by might nor by power, but by the Spirit of the Living God." The tasks are difficult, the adversaries seem to have more power, and there are many deficits. The only way we will accomplish what God has set before the Church is for us to be empowered by the Spirit of the Living God.

Zechariah, chapter 4, verse 7 gives us a wonderful little prayer that can help us: *"'What are you, mighty mountain? Before Zerubbabel you will become level ground.'"*

Next time there is some huge mountain in front of you that seems overwhelming, ungodly, immoral, wicked, or extraordinarily dark, you can say, "Before the Spirit of God, you will become level ground." You don't have to tell anybody. Just quietly start to walk around with that prayer, "You're going to become level ground." That disease will become level ground. That threat is going to become level ground. That broken heart is going to become level ground.

The same hands that began your story will complete it, because the Spirit of God is in you. He called us out of darkness, and He will see us into His Kingdom. What He has begun in us, He will bring to completion. We are strangers here, pilgrims in the world on a temporary assignment—but rest assured, we have good help along the way.

LET'S PRAY

Heavenly Father, give me a vision of Your purposes and power. I thank You that You will make the mountainous challenges I face into level ground, including ______________. I praise You for all You will do, Lord, and I thank You for Your faithfulness to me. I pray in the name of my Lord and Savior, Jesus Christ. Amen.

SECTION THREE

INVITING GOD'S BEST INTO OUR LIVES

11 CHAPTER ELEVEN

ALIGNING OUR HEARTS

As we talk about angels, the Spirit of God, and what God is doing in the earth, my goal is to help you open doors in your life and invite God in. The angels and the Spirit of God will help us in our current circumstances, but how do we ask for their help? What does that look like in the average person's life?

Become Spiritually Clean

One of the things that will open your life to the activity of the Spirit of God is to purposefully and intentionally maintain "clean hands."

During the COVID pandemic, I bet you washed your hands more in eighteen months than in the previous eighteen years. We made homemade hand sanitizer. What we used to call "moonshine," we renamed "hand sanitizer" and poured it over our hands. It killed the virus and peeled our skin. It was good for a lot of things, but don't drink it!

Though we know how to clean ourselves physically, do we care about being clean spiritually? Do we give as much attention to our spiritual cleanliness as we do our physical appearance? I don't think so.

Psalm 24, verse 3 asks two questions we should all want to know the answers to: *"Who may ascend the mountain of the LORD? Who may stand in his holy place?"*

Verses 4 and 5 tell us the answer: *"The one who has clean hands and a pure heart, who does not trust in an idol or swear by a false God. They will receive blessing from the LORD and vindication from God their Savior."*

It's clear that having clean hands and a pure heart is not based on my opinion, nor an evaluation of your neighbors. It's between you and the Lord.

Psalm 19, verse 9 says, *"The fear of the LORD is clean, enduring forever"* (ESV®). The fear of the Lord is not a dread of God. It's a respect and a reverence for Him—holding Him in esteem and recognizing that He is not like us. He is the Creator of all things!

The fear of the Lord is clean, and the Hebrew word for "clean" is *tahor*. It describes a cleanliness and purity that reaches beyond time, touching eternity. The word *tahor* is used most frequently in the Old Testament when something was being made ritually clean so it could be used in the service of the Tabernacle or the Temple. To be ritually clean, it would usually require immersion in a *mikvah*, a ritual bath.

You and I are made clean by the blood of Jesus. A tremendous price was paid so we can be clean—but in order to have that cleanliness, we have to be willing to put our transgressions and wicked thoughts under the blood of Jesus. We do this by repenting and saying, "Lord, I was thinking the wrong way. I'm sorry. Please help me."

Many people don't discipline their thoughts and their feelings. They give them a license, and it opens their minds and their emotions to some very destructive things. Though our behaviors may look good, when we don't keep our thoughts and our emotions in a clean place, we leave a way for the enemy to introduce torment into our lives. We'll talk about this more, later in the book. In the meantime, let's pray:

Lord, I'm sorry for indulging in thoughts and activities that don't honor You. I recognize I need to follow Your standards more fully to mature in my faith. Awaken me to those standards and help me to adhere to them. Help me walk in cleanliness and purity so I can enjoy even closer fellowship with You, and so my life might be a testimony of hope and transformation to others. In Jesus' name, amen.

If you watch a toddler, everything they can put their hands on goes in their mouths. It helps them build an immune system and drives their parents nuts—it serves two purposes! But if you still act that way at eighteen, it's awkward. In a similar way, we have to grow up spiritually. Things that weren't necessarily inappropriate for us as new believers become habits or thought patterns we need to shed as we begin to grow in the Lord, gain maturity, and are entrusted with responsibility. You understand that concept because it's not just true spiritually, it's also true in leadership. If it's your first day on the job, you have a freedom that somebody who is responsible for everything that's happening in that place doesn't have.

You might be thinking, *I don't want to be a spiritual leader. I just don't want to go to Hell.* That's a good starting place, but God is calling us toward something more. Tell the Lord, "I'm sorry. I've cared so little about You. I didn't want You to intrude on my plan. I'm not sure what it would mean, but I want to present myself to You. I want to have clean hands, Lord."

Cultivate a Desire for the Things of God

The second thing you can do to open your life more fully to the purposes of God is to purposefully and intentionally cultivate a desire for the things of the Kingdom of God.

Jesus told us in Matthew, chapter 6, verses 9 and 10, "'*This, then, is how you should pray: "Our Father in heaven, hallowed be your name, your kingdom come, your will be done, on earth as it is in heaven."*'"

Before we pray for our daily bread, and before we pray for those we need to forgive, Jesus told us to pray: "God, let Your Kingdom come! Help me to see! Give me a Kingdom awareness, Lord. Help me understand what's going on in our world. It's hard to find the truth. I don't know what to believe. Help me understand Your Kingdom!"

The disciples understood this struggle. For the forty days between Jesus' resurrection and His ascension, Jesus taught them about the Kingdom of God. It made such an indelible impression upon them, they spent the rest of their lives delivering the message of the Kingdom.

Paul was recruited into that group by Jesus after the fact. If I were in charge of recruiting the apostles and disciples for the Lord, I would have wanted all of them with Jesus for the full three-year run, so they could get all the training possible. Wouldn't you? But that's not how it played out. That wasn't God's plan. Apparently, He didn't need my strategic thinking.

After He ascended to Heaven, Jesus appeared to Saul of Tarsus as he was walking along the road to Damascus. Saul hated Jesus. He hated anybody who loved Jesus. But after Jesus gained Saul's attention, he had a heart change. Saul got a new name (Paul) and learned all he needed to know—so much that we learn a huge amount about Jesus and what He accomplished for us from Paul's writings.

Paul was trained in the Hebrew Bible, schooled as a Pharisee in

Jewish and rabbinic thought. He could explain what Jesus did for us in a way that met the requirements of the Jewish law and transcended his generation. Paul brought the message of the Kingdom and the King.

In Acts, chapter 17, while Paul was in Thessalonica, there was a riot, and they were trying to find and kill him. They were unsuccessful, so they dragged some of his friends before the city officials and told them, "These men are troublemakers, causing turmoil all over the world, and they have now come here." The officials asked, "What kind of trouble are they making?" The Pharisees said, "They're all defying Caesar's decree, and they're saying there's another king—one called Jesus."

In our lives today, this might be like saying, "We will only vote for someone who stands on a policy platform that honors my King, and His name is Jesus." When you bring Jesus into the conversation and declare He is the One who rules over all, it can make some people upset. But that's been true since Jesus arrived on the scene over 2,000 years ago. As Christ-followers, we live in a kingdom on earth, but we're also a part of a heavenly Kingdom. Both are inseparable from our King.

Cultivate Faithfulness

So, we're seeking to have clean hands and a Kingdom awareness, and the third thing we need to cultivate is faithfulness. I like this because faithfulness is available to anybody. You can be powerful and be faithful to the Lord. You can be powerless and be faithful to the Lord. You can be celebrated by many and still be faithful to the Lord. Or you may be ignored by many, and you can choose to be faithful to the Lord.

In fact, if you will be faithful to the Lord where you are, God will trust you with something more significant. It's a central theme in Scripture. If you'll be faithful in little, God will entrust you with much. The ultimate expression of "little" is anything in time. If He made you the keeper of all the gold in Fort Knox, it's little compared to the opportunities ahead of you.

In Greek, the language of the New Testament, the words "faith," "faithful," "believe," and "belief" all come from the same root word. It's immediately apparent when you see them. To be a person of great belief in God is to be a faithful person. If you're not a faithful person, you're not a believer.

In Luke, chapter 16, verse 10, Jesus said, "'*Whoever can be trusted with very little can also be trusted with much, and whoever is dishonest with very little will also be dishonest with much.*'"

Some of you may think, *Well, I can just cheat around the edges now, but when all the other things happen, I'll do what's right.* Or you may think, *When I win the lottery, I'll be generous.* No, you won't! The truth is if you're selfish broke, you'll be selfish rich. It's never enough. And if you think, *I'll be faithful later*, you won't. Now is the day of salvation. You're not going to find a faithful muscle later. In fact, the more you practice unfaithfulness or unrighteousness, the stronger those muscles get. I believe in repentance and mercy—I believe that the prodigal can change—but you don't want to bet your future on being the prodigal. You can practice faithfulness right where you are. It's not dependent on somebody else. Start by being faithful today, exactly where God placed you.

In Zechariah, chapter 4, verse 10, an angel tells the prophet, *"Do not despise these small beginnings, for the LORD rejoices to see the work begin"* (NLT®).

The angel is saying to the prophet, "Celebrate! If God has given you something small to do, it's because He's got something big for you to do!"

There was a time when I mowed the grass, cleaned the bathrooms, and mopped the sanctuary at our church—we couldn't afford carpet. From time to time, I would preach, too. By that point, I'd earned a couple degrees, and there I was, mowing the grass in the hot, humid July heat for a church with a handful of people. While I mowed the grass, I would get hot physically and hot spiritually. I said a lot of things to the Lord. At the time, it felt like such a long season. In retrospect, it was very brief—more than a summer and more than a year, but a very brief time. It helped prepare me for what was ahead.

You might say, "I've been faithful in small things for a long time! Nothing is changing!" I understand. It may be that the fullness of your reward won't be evident until eternity. I promise, when you get to eternity, you'll be okay with that!

To summarize, three things that you can cultivate to align your heart with what God is doing in the earth are:

- a desire for clean hands
- an awareness of the King and the Kingdom you are yielded to
- a desire to be faithful

Each of those are within you and are readily available. They don't rely on your IQ, your education, your resources, your family circumstances, or your health. They come to you when you choose to value and pursue them.

Your Integrity Gives You Credibility

One more thought: When you are giving someone a message, if you have to say, "The Lord told me," you're probably better off just being quiet. If you're a person of character and integrity, tacking on "the Lord told me" does not add credibility. I'm not saying the Lord doesn't speak into your life or give you an awareness, but there are very few times the outcome is better when you say, "the Lord said." When you play that authority card, what can the other person say? You don't have to be a rocket scientist to understand that it's manipulative.

In turn, don't be manipulated by people telling you what the Lord said. Instead, listen to the Lord. If there's a message He wants you to hear, He will confirm it or tell you Himself!

God is moving in the earth in a way that's unprecedented in our lifetimes. I want to be a part, and I know you do, too. Don't be discouraged, sad, or frightened—lift up your head! The King is coming! The angels are busy—more than 10,000 times 10,000 of them. Some of them are mighty, some are powerful, some have authority over the waters, some will bind the Dragon and throw him into the pit. God is busy! Let's get in there with Him!

LET'S PRAY

May the Lord of Hosts hear my prayers. Forgive me if I have turned away from You and imagined I could secure my own future. I humbly ask for Your direction. I submit myself as a learner, a child needing instruction. Cleanse my heart and open it to understand Your Kingdom and Your ways. Give me a willing spirit to cooperate with Your direction and cultivate faithfulness. Grant me the boldness I need to stand against the darkness. Send Your angels to do battle on my behalf. May I see Your victory in the midst of this season. Look upon me with mercy and grace. In Jesus' name, amen.

12 CHAPTER TWELVE

OPENING THE DOOR EVEN MORE

We've spent quite a bit of time talking about angels and the spiritual forces of the Kingdom of God that are released in the earth to help us. We talked in the last chapter about aligning our hearts with God and inviting Him in. The next question is this: How do we continue to open our lives and our hearts more fully to what God would do? What more do we need to know?

We know how to attend church. We understand the Ten Commandments and that we shouldn't murder. We have some idea of what immorality is and that we should avoid it. But how can we open our lives *more* fully to God and His purposes? I want all of the angelic help available. If there are mighty angels who know my address, I want them to come on in! They can bring their friends! I'm all in. How about you?

In the last chapter, I gave you some ideas that can help you begin to extend those invitations and open doors: having clean hands, a pure heart, an awareness of a King and a Kingdom, and a willingness to be faithful in the small things. I'd like to add a few more items to that list.

Be a Person Who Prays and Worships

The first has to do with prayer and worship—and I'm not really talking about when the music plays at church.

Determine to be a person who prays. You don't have to pray elaborate prayers. You can start with the prayer Jesus taught you to pray in Matthew, chapter 6, and continue to pray that until it comes alive in you:

> *"Our Father in heaven, hallowed be your name, your kingdom come, your will be done, on earth as it is in heaven. Give us today our daily bread. And forgive us our debts, as we also have forgiven our debtors. And lead us not into temptation, but deliver us from the evil one."*
>
> MATTHEW 6:9-13

You can also pray one-sentence prayers as you go about your day: "God, help me." "Teach me to value truth." "Holy Spirit, You are welcome in my life." Offering simple prayers like these can transform your prayer life.

Decide to be a person who prays.

The attitude of your heart matters when you pray, and you express that attitude in your posture. When you bow your head, it's a posture of yielding, and this is true across many cultures. When you kneel, it's not a position of power or assertion. We kneel before the Lord and at times put our faces on the ground as an expression of humility before Him.

Worshiping is also important, and it starts inside you. Worshiping is about acknowledging that God is not like you and putting yourself in a posture—an attitude—that is open to receive from Him.

I'm uncomfortable with what we call a "worship movement." I'm happy for some of the choruses that have been written, the music and the creativity around it, but worship starts in our hearts, before we ever face a community of people. If you don't ever worship privately, you're not really prepared to worship in public.

Practice Obedience

In addition to making prayer and worship a more significant part of your life, another way to open the door to God is obedience. I don't mean just keeping the rules. It's about investing your thoughts, time, energy, and efforts in the things of God. Obedience really can't be separated from service.

In the book of Matthew, Jesus shares a parable to show us whom God will reward:

> *"Who then is the faithful and wise servant, whom the master has put in charge of the servants in his household to give them their food at the proper time? It will be good for that servant whose master finds him doing so when he returns."*
>
> MATTHEW 24:45-46

What will these servants be found doing? Giving food to the people who are about God's business. Food prep, clean up, and dishwashing are not the most exciting jobs, but Jesus said, "It will be really good if you're found doing those seemingly insignificant things, when God decides to take inventory."

Verse 47 shows us the reward for our obedience: "'*Truly I tell you, he will put him in charge of all his possessions.*'" When you see the little phrase, "truly I tell you" or "I tell you the truth," it means the follow-up is going to be bizarre and unexpected. Who is going to be in charge in the Kingdom of God? The people who were faithful in the little things.

There are times I have to stand in visible places. I'm willing to do that, but the little things are important. I work hard to ensure I'm still involved in little things. Where I park my car on campus matters to me. I choose parking spots away from the building, so the close parking spaces are available for those who need them. It's not important to other people, but it matters to me because it isn't about privilege. I prefer most days to get to the office early and stay late because it isn't others I serve. It's the Lord. I don't know what little things look like for you, but if you engage in the little things with the Lord, He will give you bigger assignments.

Don't just talk about the Lord. Serve Him.

Cultivate Humility and the Fear of the Lord

There is one more thing to add to our list of actions that open the door to God's Spirit: cultivating humility and the fear of the Lord.

Proverbs, chapter 15, verse 33 says, "*The fear of the LORD is the instruction of wisdom, and before honor is humility*" (NKJV®). This verse doesn't describe a dread of God but a respect, a reverence, and a yielding to Him. We are not like Him. He is different from us. He created this place. He created 100 million angels. He knows the ending at the beginning. He's not like us, and yet we're often so resistant to Him and His plans. We say, "Well, I'm not going to let Him tell me what to do." We want God to be interested in how *we* feel, but we are not as concerned with how *He* feels.

We're like preschoolers. They don't care if you're tired; they still ask, "Don't you want to play? Oh, come on, get out of the chair. Come play with me!" Isn't that kind of how we feel with the Lord? "Don't You want to play with me? Come on. Do what I want You to do! It'll be great!" But we need to cultivate the fear of the Lord, so we're prepared to follow *His* plans for us.

We also need humility. Proverbs, chapter 22, verse 4 says, *"Humility is the fear of the LORD; its wages are riches and honor and life."*

You don't get humility online. No one will deliver it to your door. Humility is acquired indirectly. When you serve others, you cultivate a little bit of humility. When you think of others as valuable, you cultivate a little humility. When you take your time and energy to open your Bible and say, "God, I would like to know about You," you're expressing humility to Him.

I've given you a short list of things to start to cultivate:

- Be a person who prays and worships.
- Practice obedience.
- Pursue humility and the fear of the Lord.

These things will increase your ability to recognize your intersection with the angels. They will help you begin to hear the Spirit of God more clearly and understand His Kingdom. In the season ahead of us, we're going to need that! There is a spiritual war going on, but you have an army by your side! Something good is coming to you.

Give Thanks and Forgive

Let's take a few minutes to put some of these ideas into practice by giving thanks to the Lord. Tell Him what you're thankful for today. We have food to eat, clothing, and shelter, and our children have schools and health care available to them. We have so many freedoms. We have so much. I understand the world is not just. I'm not asking you to think about all that is wrong. I'm asking you to take a few minutes to give thanks to the Lord for who He is and all He has done and is doing for you.

I also want to ask you to do something that releases enormous spiritual power into your life: forgive. Decide right now not to leave this chapter harboring any anger, resentment, bitterness, or hatred. This means not looking for something in exchange for forgiving—no payback, no apologies, and no judgment.

We'll start our prayer by simply saying "thank You," and then we're going to forgive. Sometimes I like to pray with my hands up or by kneeling. I want the Lord to know I intend to yield to Him. You can find whatever posture feels appropriate to you, then let's pray.

LET'S PRAY

Lord, I want to thank You for Your goodness and Your mercy to me. You love me. You called me out of darkness. You have forgiven my sins. You have blessed my life in so many ways. Father, I'm free to worship, and I thank You for it today. I

worship You and give You glory, honor, and praise because You are worthy.

Forgive me for when I have been reluctant, stubborn, rebellious, selfish, disinterested, and distracted. Father, I come today in humility. Begin to give me listening ears, an open heart, and eyes to see. Give me understanding beyond myself. Lord, thank You that, in spite of all the things I'm not and the struggles I face, You are sovereign over all. I give You glory, Lord Jesus, for what You have done for me and for the sacrifices You've made. Almighty God, thank You that You're willing to be my Heavenly Father and watch over me. Holy Spirit, thank You that You lead, guide, direct, teach, train, and convict me. You are worthy of all glory, honor, and praise!

Lord, I want to take a moment to forgive. I've been hurt and disappointed. I've been mistreated. Lord, I have the wounds and scars that come from a journey through a broken world. As You have been gracious to forgive me, today, in obedience to You, I choose to forgive. I release anyone of anything. I specifically forgive __________ for ____________. I cancel the debt and set them free, releasing them today into Your great mercy. I'm not open for further mistreatment, but I thank You that I don't have to carry the weight of unforgiveness any longer. As I release them, I ask You to release me. Lord, let the anger, the resentment, and the bitterness go. May any physical limits that have come to me because of those things be broken over my life. Restore my health, my peace, and my contentment.

Lord, I thank You, and I release these people now, in Jesus' name. I set them free, through the blood of Jesus. Thank You for the deliverance that is mine, and that I am no longer burdened with frustration, anger, and hostility. I praise You that the blood of Jesus has redeemed me out of the hand of the enemy and has settled all my accounts. In Jesus' name, amen.

SECTION FOUR

WHAT ARE WE FIGHTING?

13 CHAPTER THIRTEEN

LEARNING TO OVERCOME

I hope focusing on the angels has broadened your hope, mind, and awareness of their role in the heavenly realms and our physical world. Just thinking about the number of angels involved with us is astounding. Let me take a minute to summarize some of the things we've discussed so far. Jesus said He could call as many as twelve legions of angels. Since 3,000 to 6,000 is a legion, there could have been 70,000 or more angels assigned to help Jesus! In just one snapshot in the book of Revelation, we see 100 million angels. The Bible also says that the angels of the children have the Father's attention, so there's an angel attached to each child. The number of angels is getting up there!

There are mighty angels, strong angels, powerful angels, and angels with assignments to various regions of the earth and various groups of people in the earth. I have no doubt there's a myriad of angels around us and with us right now! Angels aren't there as some abstract ethereal creation of God the Father—they're there because we need them! I've come to the conclusion that God is practical—eminently more practical than I would ever be. If there are angels in that quantity, sent to be ministering spirits and messengers on our behalf, it's because we need them.

Now I want to take some time to look at the reason why we need that help. I don't want to glorify or draw unnecessary attention to it, but to be aware of the angels and not be aware of what they're standing against seems amazingly naive to me.

It's a bit more fashionable to believe in angels than it is to believe in the Devil and demons. If you say you believe in angels, you're kind of cool. You can find secular people who say, "Oh yeah, I believe in angels." But if you tell them you believe in the Devil and demons, many people will take a step back. But the more we understand our adversary and the way he functions, the better prepared we will be to fight against his dark realm. Let's take the time to learn a little bit about the attitude and posture we'll need to hold in order to be triumphant in our assignments.

Jesus Addressed Demons

We'll start by discussing unclean spirits, and I can't think of a better place to start than with Jesus' ministry in Mark, chapter 1. Mark was the first Gospel written, and it is the shortest of the four Gospels. Scholars almost universally agree that Matthew and Luke had the book of Mark as a reference when they wrote their Gospels.

I don't believe it's accidental that the Gospel of Mark begins with an account of a man who was demonized. Dealing with demons was a very prominent part of Jesus' ministry. Before we get too deep into this part of the book, and as you're trying to make a decision about whether you're going to believe or not, I would point out to you that Jesus not only believed in the existence of demons, He addressed them! If Jesus believed in them, I'm just going to climb out on a limb and suggest maybe we should, too. Jesus understood that demons influenced people and had an impact in His world so much that He spent time and energy teaching about them. Perhaps you and I should create some space in our own discipleship journey to understand the role of demonic activity and how to respond to it.

I don't want this topic to make you feel frightened, weird, or strange. Strange is not spiritual. Strange is just strange. My goal is to offer practical information that is necessary to live as informed and effective Christ-followers.

In the beginning of Mark, Jesus and His disciples went into Capernaum. When Jesus began His public ministry, He moved from Nazareth, a little village in the hills of Galilee, to Capernaum, a fishing village on the north end of the Sea of Galilee. The most valuable resource in the Middle East was fresh water, and the Sea of Galilee is the largest freshwater resource in the region. If you had a message you wanted to communicate, you'd want to deliver your message on a busy road near that water source—and that is exactly where Jesus went.

Mark, chapter 1, verses 21 and 22 say: "*They went into Capernaum; and immediately on the Sabbath Jesus entered the synagogue and began to teach. And they were amazed at His teaching; for He was teaching them as one having authority, and not as the scribes*" (NASB®).

There's a difference between talking *about* Scripture and talking as if Scripture *impacted our lives*. If you've spent your life talking about Scripture and studying about the Bible, I would like to invite you to a new position. Begin to think about the Bible as if it impacted your life. It's the difference between reading a cookbook and using its recipes to make a meal.

The story continues:

> *Just then there was a man in their synagogue with an unclean spirit; and he cried out, saying, "What business do you have with us, Jesus of Nazareth? Have You come to destroy us? I know who You are: the Holy One of God!" And Jesus rebuked him, saying, "Be quiet, and come out of him!" After throwing him into convulsions and crying out with a loud voice, the unclean spirit came out of him. And they were all amazed, so they debated among themselves, saying, "What is this? A new teaching with authority! He*

commands even the unclean spirits, and they obey Him."
Immediately the news about Him spread everywhere into
all the surrounding region of Galilee.

MARK 1: 23-28, NASB®

It's an intriguing introduction to me. Before Jesus begins a healing ministry, before He prays for the sick, He sets a man free from a demonic influence.

When it comes to discussing things like "demonic influence," I'd like to point out there are several words the New Testament uses interchangeably to discuss this type of spiritual presence: unclean spirit, evil spirit, demon, and demonic spirit. They're synonymous; they refer to the same thing.

In the scripture above, there are Bible translations that use the word "possessed" to describe the man, but I think that is inconsistent with the meaning of the original language. "Possession" connotes the idea that you are controlled, dominated, and under the total influence of someone. I think a more accurate representation is the man was demonized and influenced by an unclean spirit, an evil spirit, or a demonic spirit.

We've been considering the influence of angels, and it's clear they are not present in the abstract. They are there because they are engaged in a spiritual conflict.

In this scenario, a demonized man was present in the synagogue.

He appeared to be a faithful Jewish man who was living under the provisions of the covenant available to him—he was in the synagogue on the Sabbath, after all. He wasn't windsurfing on the lake! Even with those practices in place, he was subjected to demonic influence. We would like to pretend that, because we're Christian or going to church, we're not subjected to evil influences, but that's not a biblical perspective.

Demons Recognize Jesus

In verse 24, the unclean spirit who was harassing the man said to Jesus, "'*What business do you have with us, Jesus of Nazareth? Have You come to destroy us? I know who You are: the Holy One of God*'" (NASB®). The unclean spirit understood who Jesus was before the rabbi, the new disciples, or anyone else did! This encounter took place early in Jesus' ministry, and at that point in time, no one really knew the extent of who Jesus was. They might have known the village He came from, but that was the sum of their insight. This means the spiritual influences around us have some insight, understanding, and awareness we may not have. That's not my opinion. It's biblical.

In this passage, we see the unclean spirit responds when there's an authority present greater than itself. It tells Jesus, "I know who You are." And when Jesus said, "You've got to go," the demon understood it had to leave, and it objected. It didn't leave without adding some further humiliation to the man, sending him into convulsions, but it left.

It's important to note that the unclean spirit was antagonistic to Jesus. The nature of the interaction was one of antagonism and conflict. I think we need to recognize there are spiritual forces active in the earth that stand in opposition to the purposes of God in your life. You need to not only be aware of that but also have an intentional way to respond.

Protect Your Spiritual Immune System

God designed you with a very elaborate immune system with many layers. It's amazingly effective, helping you overcome challenges you may never know about. But occasionally, through some weakness or opening in your immune system, bacteria, a virus, or something else will impact your physical health and well-being, and you'll need a plan so you can overcome the illness. In a similar way, you have a spiritual immune system. If you give attention to it and watch over it, it does a remarkable job of protecting you from any number of things. We are all subject to the influences of unclean spirits, and we need a plan to help us stay spiritually healthy.

We've talked a lot about how angels are ministering spirits sent here to assist us. They are messengers sent to help us understand God's perspective with greater clarity. We've looked at multiple examples where angels have taken roles in the lives of individuals and brought them strength, encouragement, or hope.

In the same way, we need to recognize the impact of these unclean spirits. They come to torment, diminish, humiliate, and destroy you. It's not a casual thing. You can't afford to say, "I just don't believe in that." That's like saying, "I just don't believe in viruses." Unclean spirits are real, and it's worth taking the time and effort to pay attention to what Scripture tells us about them.

LET'S PRAY

Heavenly Father, if there is anything unclean within me, help me to recognize it. Help me to see the destruction it's bringing into my life. Lord, I repent of and renounce all that separates me from You including ____________________. I turn away from it, and I confess it was wrong. I accept Your grace, Your love, and Your mercy. Help me to learn to walk in a way that honors You. In Jesus' name, amen.

Learn to Stand

As we approach the End of the Age, the Bible clearly tells us there will be unprecedented activity amongst those unclean spirits. Our adversaries know they are approaching the end of their time, and there's a sense of desperation. The last two minutes of a football game take longer than the whole previous part of the half, right? If you're waiting for someone to finish watching the game, you have time to bathe, shave, and put the kids to bed, because there's an intensity, a focus, and an intentionality that comes in those last two minutes. Every movement that happens becomes important. The End of the Age will be like that. There's a heightened significance to everything that happens, as it all comes to a culmination.

I think that's why God has begun to prepare us with the shaking in our world. He's getting our attention and teaching us to refocus, so we can understand where our true security rests. He is leading us to reimagine our lives a little bit, to help us develop strength. We're having to learn how to stand in ways we've never had to stand before. We've imagined that our futures could be secured by the Bill of Rights, the Constitution, truth, or all sorts of things that seem to have been called into question. We're having to learn to stand and trust God for our futures, and it's awkward and uncomfortable. Some are trying to ignore it, some are just whistling along as if it weren't happening, and some are learning to stand.

I'd like to encourage you to learn to stand, and when we talk about standing, it is not just defensive. It's not just an endurance contest. It's not just about perseverance. We have two primary choices: We can be an overcomer, or we can be overcome. In Scripture, I don't see a third option. There's not a neutral place.

LET'S PRAY

Heavenly Father, give me boldness to stand for Your truth. Give me discernment, so I might see as You see. Deliver us from evil. May Your Kingdom come and Your will be done on Earth. In Jesus' name, amen.

Choose to Be an Overcomer

Romans, chapter 12, verse 21 says, *"Do not be overcome by evil, but overcome evil with good."* Overcoming is not just hanging on. It's not just an endurance contest. Overcoming means we intend to have victory over evil, not just resist it. We need to expand our definition!

When Jesus said in Matthew, chapter 16, verse 18, *"I will build my church, and the gates of Hades will not overcome it,"* the most common form of warfare was siege warfare. Important cities were defended by enormous stone walls built to protect them from invading armies. When there was a threat, you'd lock the gates of the city—and the most vulnerable part of a walled city was the gates. The gates were typically made of wood that could be burned or broken with a battering ram. If you could breach the gates, you could overcome the city.

So, when Jesus said the gates of Hell would not prevail against the Church, He didn't describe a Church being besieged. He described a Church that is assertive and on the offense; Hell is withstanding the assault of the Church. We need an emotional change, a heart change, and a change in our thoughts. We're not just hanging on against the forces of evil. There's an innumerable company of angels at work on our behalf, and Jesus said the gates of Hell will not prevail against us—the Church.

Remember, in Romans it says to not be overcome by evil, but overcome evil—not with politicians, political parties, or ideologies—but with good. That's going to take us right back to God because He is the only One who is good.

It's important to understand the nature of this conflict so we don't feel frightened or threatened. You also shouldn't be arrogant or flippant. On your own, you are no match for the Devil. The Bible is filled with stories of our heroes being tripped up by our adversary. If you can't remember, think of Moses the murderer or David the adulterer. This conflict is not something flippant or casual—we're going to be overcomers, or we're going to be overcome.

As we discussed, when the book of Revelation was written, it began with letters to the seven churches in Asia minor, which is modern-day Turkey. Jesus' message to each church is similar: He diagnoses their condition, offers a remedy for where there are weaknesses, and then provides instructions on how to finish their course.

Revelation, chapter 2, verse 7 says, *"He who has an ear, let him hear what the Spirit says to the churches. To him who overcomes I will give to eat from the tree of life, which is in the midst of the Paradise of God"* (NKJV®).

Verse 11 says, *"He who has an ear, let him hear what the Spirit says to the churches. He who overcomes shall not be hurt by the second death"* (NKJV®).

Verse 17 says, *"He who has an ear, let him hear what the Spirit says to the churches. To him who overcomes, I will give some of the hidden manna to eat"* (NKJV®).

Verse 26 says, *"The one who overcomes, and the one who keeps My deeds until the end, I will give him authority over the nations"* (NASB®).

What is the one consistent prerequisite? Being an overcomer!

Now, I think in contemporary Christendom, we would rather be overlookers than overcomers. Overcoming suggests engagement, acknowledgement, recognition, and skin in the game. Overlooking is more of the ostrich approach—hear no evil, see no evil, do no evil.

LET'S PRAY

Thank You, Lord, that You have placed me at this pivotal point in the unfolding story of humanity to be an ambassador for You. Help me fulfill that assignment well—with enthusiasm, diligence, and joy. Father, without Your help, there is no hope. But with You, I am an overcomer. I have a living hope, and His name is Jesus. In His name, amen.

The Importance of Truth

One of the challenges we face right now in our culture is that "truth has fallen in the streets," to borrow the words of the prophet Isaiah. Truth is not held in high esteem. There's a spiritual battle raging underneath the surface. Because truth is not valued, very influential people can make a presentation, speech, or report that is absolutely fabricated, and then there will be a large group of people saying, "Oh, that was wonderful!" It's like the emperor's new clothes. People are overlooking what's obvious.

The truth is often inconvenient, uncomfortable, and awkward. So, we think: *Don't ask. Let's not talk about it.* But we're called to be overcomers, and that means we need to have an accurate diagnosis. We have to be willing to look at the truth.

This begins by telling the truth about ourselves and acknowledging where we are. Don't avoid the challenges you have, the temptations you face, the places where you emotionally struggle, or where your thought life is not easy. We need to tell the truth because if we acknowledge our reality, we can overcome it, we can repair it, we can forgive, and we can choose a new path.

If we just choose to be overlookers, we remove ourselves completely from the arena. We become like that unfaithful servant who buried his talents, or we become like the bridesmaids who were unprepared as they waited for the bridegroom. Our assignment is to be overcomers, and that's not a passive response to life.

LET'S PRAY

Almighty God, I choose to align myself with Your Truth and yield to You in obedience. Forgive me for my pride and rebellion. Holy Spirit, teach me to walk uprightly and give me an understanding heart. Deliver me from anything that distracts me from Your purposes for my life. May Your Kingdom come,

and Your will fill the entire Earth. In Jesus' name, amen.

Consider the Apostle Paul

Most would agree that Paul had a relatively effective run as a servant of Jesus, even after his bumpy beginning. Two millennia after his death, his faith still impacts the world.

We find Paul near the end of his life in 2 Timothy, chapter 4. He had already been on trial for his life once and narrowly escaped condemnation to death, and as he awaited his second trial, the outcome seemed dire. From a jail cell in Rome, he wrote a letter to Timothy, a young man he had mentored.

I want to draw your attention to the circumstances he was in because by every secular evaluation, he was an abject failure. One of the things we're going to have to address, as we walk through this spiritual conflict, is who defines success in your life. What standard are you using? If your standard is the same as the secular world, you have a problem. It will lead you into some destructive choices.

Paul, by almost every professional evaluation, is not doing well. He writes to Timothy:

> *Do your best to come to me quickly, for Demas, because he loved this world, has deserted me and has gone to Thessalonica. Crescens has gone to Galatia, and Titus to Dalmatia. Only Luke is with me. Get Mark and bring him*

with you, because he is helpful to me in my ministry. I sent Tychicus to Ephesus.

2 TIMOTHY 4:9-12

His leadership seemed a little squishy. He couldn't even keep his team together.

He continues in verse 13, *"When you come, bring the cloak that I left with Carpus at Troas, and my scrolls, especially the parchments."*

This verse makes me emotional every time I read it. I think of the people who have mentored me in my life, those who have spoken into my spiritual life and its development. If I received a text message from one of them that said, "Could you hurry to where I am? I'm cold and I'm hungry, and there's nobody to help me," I know what that would stir on the inside of me.

Paul continues his letter:

Alexander the metalworker did me a great deal of harm. The Lord will repay him for what he has done. You too should be on your guard against him, because he strongly opposed our message. At my first defense, no one came to my support, but everyone deserted me.

2 TIMOTHY 4:14-16

Paul was in Rome. There was a church and believers in Rome, but they were treating Paul as if he were toxic. He had been victimized by the cancel culture. Nobody wanted to stand next to him. He was out there on the end of the plank by himself. He wrote to Timothy and asked him to hurry because the last time he had to stand on that public dock, nobody stood with him except the Lord, who, verse 17 tells us, *"stood at my side and gave me strength."*

Who do you think was also standing at his side? Some contingent of the heavenly host. I don't know if it was the same angel who strengthened Elijah in the desert, cooked him a meal and said, "You're going to need this." I don't know if it was the same angel who spoke to Paul when he was on board that ship when it was about to be destroyed and said, "You're going to make it to Rome." But God sent messengers to strengthen Paul. Verses 17 and 18 say that happened, "... *so that through [Paul], the message might be fully proclaimed and all the Gentiles might hear it. And I was delivered from the lion's mouth. The Lord will rescue me from every evil attack and will bring me safely to his heavenly kingdom. To him be glory for ever and ever. Amen."*

That doesn't sound like a defeated passage to me!

In 2 Corinthians, chapter 11, verse 24, Paul said, *"Five times I received from the Jews the forty lashes minus one."* Forty lashes from a Roman scourge was believed to kill a man. They used leather whips with metal or glass woven into the leather so it would tear the flesh off your back. Forty lashes would kill you, and five times Paul was given thirty-nine. Can you imagine the amount of scar tissue that would build up after five times? The first time, your back would be laid open to the bone with the muscles torn. It would heal, but you would be disfigured. When it happened the second time, you would be torn apart again, and your scars would be in a far worse condition than the first time. By the fifth time, I'm relatively confident he couldn't stand up straight any longer. There was too much scarring. Still, he said, "I'm confident that the Lord will bring me through." I think we can call Paul an overcomer. He wasn't passive, and he certainly wasn't an overlooker.

We've filled our churches with overlookers for so long. We overlook sin. We overlook selfishness. We overlook greed. We overlook immorality. We don't want to be critical. We don't want to be agitated, angry, or harsh. But we must change and decide to be filled with truth, compassion, grace, and the fear of the Lord. We're not going to overcome without it.

I want to point out one more thing about the encounter we discussed earlier in Mark, chapter 1. When Jesus left the synagogue, the demonized man was still there, but the demon was gone. I think we're more often in the habit of removing the man and leaving the demon in place.

God is asking us to be different in our places of work, at our schools, and in our recreational activities. We're going to have to learn to become overcomers. It's a more assertive posture. We've been overlookers long enough.

LET'S PRAY

Heavenly Father, I lift my heart and my voice to You in praise and thanksgiving. There is no one like You. From Your great mercy, I have received life and hope. I joyfully yield my life to the Lordship of Jesus. Through Him, I have overcome and am overcoming. Give me the strength to complete the course You have chosen for me. Protect me from the attacks of the enemy, and fill my heart with peace and joy. Open my eyes to see the majesty of our God and King. Let the earth be filled with the praises of our God. In Jesus' name, amen.

14 CHAPTER FOURTEEN

UNDERSTANDING OUR ENEMY

The forces that determine human history don't begin with armies, empires, rulers, or economics. From a biblical perspective, history is determined by two categories: the visible and the invisible. The visible forces that shape history are obvious. You've studied those in school. You can give a litany of those significant leaders, economic movements, great business ideas, and breakthrough inventions.

We're far less aware of the invisible forces. What I'm inviting you to imagine is you and I have influence *alongside* and *with* those invisible forces. They don't just act upon us. They are at work, exercising a continuous and decisive influence on the events in the visible realm—what happens in the world that we see, touch, and feel. In other words, the world that's available to us with our five senses is continuously acted upon by invisible forces.

This is not a reach, folks. Most of us believe the COVID virus was real. It shook the entire world, changing how we do business, go to school, travel, vacation, walk in public, and worship—and you can't see a virus. You can see the symptoms of people who are infected with the virus, but you can't see the virus itself.

We know this is true with viruses, but when the Bible invites us to believe that God, who is a Spirit, created the earth and everything in it, we say, "Well, I'm not sure I believe in those invisible things."

I'm quite happy to follow the science, but more certainly than I want to do that, I want to follow the faith. I'm going to act as if God is true, and He's told me the truth in His Word.

We see what this looks like in Colossians, chapter 4, verse 12: *"Epaphras, who is one of you and a servant of Christ Jesus, sends greetings. He is always wrestling in prayer for you."*

I don't believe this is a euphemism. I think Paul was describing the effort with which this man prayed for the church in Colossae, his city of origin. Wrestling in prayer is more than a one-sentence "let's pray" moment. Wrestling describes full contact—the most exhausting form of physical contact available to us, because the moment you relent, the moment you relax, the moment you release your tension, you're done.

Do you think of prayer that way—as a spiritual wrestling match?

Let's look at Romans, chapter 15, verse 30: *"I urge you, brothers and sisters, by our Lord Jesus Christ and by the love of the Spirit, to join me in my struggle by praying to God for me."* Here Paul essentially says, "I'm struggling, and I'm not asking you for money or to organize. I need you to pray."

Why do we need to pray? We're in a battle. Ephesians, chapter 6, verse 12 says, *"For our struggle is not against flesh and blood, but against the rulers, against the authorities, against the powers of this dark world and against the spiritual forces of evil in the heavenly realms."* The real battles of our lives are not with people, organizations, politicians, or political parties. They are against the spiritual forces of evil in the heavenly realms.

The Devil Is Actually Real

Satan is the embodiment of evil and an orchestrator of evil in the world. Jesus believed in him. In Luke, chapter 10, verse 18, Jesus said, *"I saw Satan fall like lightning from heaven."*

I've studied in some academic settings where they said, "Well, first-century people believed in demons, angels, and spirits, so some of that is reflected in the New Testament, but we're far more enlightened than that now." That thought fills our theological schools and informs a number of pulpits today. Many of us are reluctant to acknowledge the Devil because we think it diminishes our intellect, or in some way steps away from the education and the thought patterns we worked to establish. But accepting a premise like that diminishes Jesus' words and makes a mockery of His story.

Jesus came, as a revelation of the Father, to give us insight into our world and how to be a participant in the Kingdom of God. Jesus believes the Devil exists—so I will, too.

We behave as if we are just too educated or sophisticated to be influenced by the Devil. If that doesn't work, we try to believe that maybe our denomination—or the congregation where we worship—is too enlightened to be caught up in a discussion about evil. It's just unseemly. After all, today we have psychology. I'm not opposed to psychology, but to imagine that the study of psychology removes the influence of evil spirits would be like saying studying biology removes a virus.

Maybe we just prefer to say those things don't bother us in our country. We believe those kinds of spiritual forces exist, but they're a part of someplace else—maybe less developed nations or areas with a little less sophistication—places where the people believe in voodoo and other strange things. Evil like that doesn't bother us here.

But suppose I put you in charge of evil, and you had the assignment to distribute the forces of evil across the world. Would you focus on the remotest places on the planet, the places that had little means of communication or influence? Or would you focus your demonic forces on the centers of wealth and power? Because if you could change thoughts in those places, you could influence the entire planet! I think you know where you would focus those forces.

There are also people who say, "I just don't believe there is a Devil." Well, bless your heart! I would join you if disbelief would change the reality. You can say, "I don't believe in gravity," but if you step off the edge of the roof of your house, you'll rapidly fall to the ground. Remaining ignorant of the Devil does not make him disappear.

Satan Rules a Kingdom

There is a Devil, and he rules a kingdom, just as certainly as God reigns over a Kingdom. But these two kingdoms are not equal in power or magnitude—and that's an important thing to remember.

When Paul talks about what we're battling in Ephesians, chapter 6, he describes a hierarchical order to the kingdom of darkness in the same way there's a structure to the Kingdom of God. In God's Kingdom, there are archangels and angels with realms of authority. In the kingdom of darkness, there's also a hierarchy. Satan is a great imitator, and he imitated the order he saw God create.

I think it's worth stopping for a minute to fully recognize this fact: Satan truly does rule a kingdom. This is not fiction, nor is it a subtle theme of Scripture.

Ephesians, chapter 2, verses 1 and 2 say: *"As for you, you were dead in your transgressions and sins, in which you used to live when you followed the ways of this world and of the ruler of the kingdom of the air, the spirit who is now at work in those who are disobedient."* Here, Satan is described as the ruler of the kingdom of the air. The kingdom he presides over has its seat of authority somewhere between God's Heaven and Earth.

The Bible talks about three heavens, and the word "heaven" in Genesis, chapter 1 is plural. I tend to think of it as three layers in a cake, but rather than thinking of them just stacked in a layer, think about them as different dimensions. Satan is the ruler of one of those dimensions—the kingdom of the air—and he clearly has access to what's happening in the earth.

He began his journey in the Kingdom of God, but he led a rebellion against God, and a third of the angels joined him. That's a significant number, especially when you consider what you know about angels. There were more than 70,000 angels as a part of Jesus' personal escort. In one snapshot in the book of Revelation, there are 100 million angels. Every child in the world has an angel with direct access to the Father's attention. That's a significant number of angels—and those are just the angels who honor and obey the Lord. When Satan rebelled against God, a third of the total angels went with him. So, there are lot of angels on the dark side as well, and Satan rules over them.

Satan's Power in Our World

In the book of John, Jesus refers to Satan as the prince of this world, and that's a title of authority:

"Now is the time for judgment on this world; now the prince of this world will be driven out. And I, when I am lifted up from the earth, will draw all people to myself." He said this to show the kind of death he was going to die.

JOHN 12:31-33

First John, chapter 2, verse 15, talks about the realm we currently live in: *"Do not love the world or anything in the world."* When the New Testament talks about "the world," it's not talking about a ball of matter hurtling through space. It's talking about the present world order. When Jesus comes back, He's going to rule and reign on planet Earth. You're not going to spend all eternity in Heaven sitting on a cloud listening to an endless succession of preachers. Jesus is going to rule and reign in a new Heaven and a new Earth, and this present world order is going to pass away. It's temporary.

John continues his advice for us:

If anyone loves the world, love for the Father is not in them. For everything in the world—the lust of the flesh, the lust of the eyes, and the pride of life—comes not from the Father but from the world. The world and its desires pass away, but whoever does the will of God lives forever.

1 JOHN 2:15-17

A simple thing we can deduce from that portion of Scripture

is that Satan's kingdom is not eternal because his kingdom is enmeshed in this present age. When this age comes to a conclusion, his role will also come to an end, and he will be judged by God Himself. The closer we come to the End of the Age—and I believe we are approaching it—the more feverishly Satan will respond.

Prepare for Combat

Satan was defeated through Jesus' death, burial, and resurrection, but you and I are deployed in the midst of this conflict because Jesus' victory has not yet been fully established in time. We still need to be prepared for combat.

Second Corinthians, chapter 10, verse 4 says, *"The weapons we fight with are not the weapons of the world. On the contrary, they have divine power to demolish strongholds."* In Christ, we have the power of Heaven to demolish strongholds—but Heaven is waiting for us to engage, to become overcomers, to wrestle in prayer, and to take up the struggle.

First Corinthians, chapter 9, verse 24 says, *"Do you not know that in a race all the runners run, but only one gets the prize? Run in such a way as to get the prize."* Today, everybody gets a participation trophy, but this is written during the first century, and Paul is telling the Corinthians to run in such a way as to get the prize. Don't do it casually. Then, verses 26 and 27 say, *"Therefore I do not run like someone running aimlessly; I do not fight like a boxer beating the air. No, I strike a blow to my body and make it my slave so that after I have preached to others, I myself will not be disqualified for the prize."*

What's missing in Paul's language was presumption. He was not saying, "I'm the great apostle! I met Jesus on the road to Damascus, and this is my curriculum vitae and the miracles I've seen." Instead, what he said was, "I keep myself under strict discipline because I don't want to have shared the good news and then miss its benefit. I'm going to overcome."

Paul tells us he's not like a man running aimlessly. He's living on purpose. In the same chapter he said, "You've all been to the stadium and have seen the athletes race. Everyone runs, but only one wins. Run to win."

All good athletes train hard for a gold medal that tarnishes and fades. You're after one that's gold eternally. The difficulties we walk through present the opportunity to develop a reward that far exceeds the discomfort or displeasure that takes place in time. Second Corinthians, chapter 4, verses 17 and 18 say, *"For our light and momentary troubles are achieving for us an eternal glory that far outweighs them all. So we fix our eyes not on what is seen, but on what is unseen, since what is seen is temporary, but what is unseen is eternal."*

How do you look at something you cannot see? We're going to have to learn to look with something other than just our physical senses. We're going to need a God-perspective.

The Devil's principal ways of influencing your life are in your mind, thoughts, and emotions. You need to be aware there are evil spirits who can influence your emotions. Not every emotion you have is godly. People might say, "You can't tell me how I feel." That's true, but I can tell you some feelings are ungodly. They may be your feelings, but if you own those feelings, they're going to take you to a destructive place. You need to be aware of and prepared for the enemy's attacks.

Satan Can Cause Physical Ailments

Before Luke got into the writing business, his day job was a physician. He traveled with Paul, and Lord knows, Paul needed a traveling physician—he consistently faced physical challenges and suffering. In Luke, chapter 13, Jesus was in a synagogue on a Sabbath. Verse 11 says, *"A woman was there who had been crippled by a spirit for eighteen years. She was bent over and could not straighten up at all."* That's an important sentence from the physician: There was a woman who was physically impaired because of the presence of an unclean spirit. Does that mean every physical impairment is caused by an unclean spirit? No, but it introduces the possibility that some are. How would you know the difference? We have to know more about unclean spirits. Don't be afraid—ask the Spirit of God to help you discern.

As the story continues, Jesus acknowledges the woman and heals her. It makes the audience in the synagogue angry—they chose to categorize the healing as "work." You're not allowed to work on the Sabbath, so in their eyes, Jesus had broken a Sabbath rule. Jesus was angry with them because they cared more about their rules than they did about people, and we see His response in verse 16: "'*Then should not this woman, a daughter of Abraham, whom Satan has kept bound for eighteen long years, be set free on the Sabbath day from what bound her?*'"

Jesus' description of this woman is important to you and me. The Covenant that is available to her is the Covenant God made with Abraham. Jesus doesn't say this woman is in a battle with an evil spirit because of her immorality or her ungodliness. He simply says this woman, living in the full light of the Covenant available to her, is struggling with the intrusion of an unclean spirit. You see, it's more popular in the contemporary Church to say, "Unclean spirits, evil spirits, and demonic spirits are all synonymous in the New Testament, and they wouldn't bother a Christian." If that's the case, why are we told to put on the armor of God in Ephesians, chapter 6? We create these little theological loopholes so we don't have to think about the awkward truths of Scripture.

In Luke, chapter 9, we find a story about a desperate father and his son. In verses 39 to 40, the father tells Jesus, "'*A spirit seizes him and he suddenly screams; it throws him into convulsions so that he foams at the mouth. It scarcely ever leaves him and is destroying him. I begged your disciples to drive it out, but they could not.*'" Do you hear the desperation in the father? He's saying, "I've done everything I know to do. I've brought my son to strangers and admitted my son's problems, the weaknesses in my family system, and my powerlessness to help my son." That is not a comfortable thing to admit in a public setting. And then you hear the despair, "After I did all that, Your disciples couldn't help him." This man is beyond the end of his rope.

Jesus replies in verse 41, "'*You unbelieving and perverse generation … how long shall I stay with you and put up with you?*'" Jesus is not mad at the father—He's looking at His disciples. Jesus continues in verses 41 and 42, "'*Bring your son here.' Even while the boy was coming, the demon threw him to the ground in a convulsion. But Jesus rebuked the impure spirit, healed the boy and gave him back to his father.*" Jesus rebuked the spirit that had tormented the boy and caused physical implications. That doesn't mean every time you have some physical response, there is a demon attached to it—but it does introduce the possibility.

If we're going to walk in the light of Scripture, we're going to have to make room in our imaginations that there are forces arrayed against us more powerful than a virus and more significant than bacteria—because those things can only destroy our physical shell. Jesus told us, "There are forces arrayed against you that are far more powerful than those, and those are the ones you should really be concerned about."

Satan's Influence Affects More than One Person

Those spiritual influences and the impact of those spiritual things are very seldom limited just to an individual. Once spiritual forces are unleashed, they typically impact a family, a family system, a family tree, generations, and communities. This is true for both good and evil.

We see this throughout the Bible. Jonah preached in Nineveh, and the entire city repented. The people in Jerusalem, when presented with Jesus and the opportunity to acknowledge who He was, shouted in the streets, "Crucify Him!" Everybody in the city didn't scream that. In reality, it was a relatively small percentage of the population—a few hundred, perhaps a few thousand people. Most of the people were busy. Kids were playing soccer. They were planning cookouts for the evening—but that group of people who stood in the streets and shouted, "Crucify Him!" brought a consequence on the whole city.

I want you to know there's value in your life and the choices you make. There's a significance to your life that reaches far beyond your income, your balance sheet, your education, and the people who you think care about your opinion. Almighty God cares about your opinion. Your choices for good or for evil—to be an overcomer or to be overcome—have enormous influence. Almighty God knows your name!

Spiritual influences can extend to families, tribes, communities, and even whole nations. Once they're released, they'll continue from generation to generation until something happens to cancel their efforts.

The Spiritual World Impacts Our Physical World

Most of the things we observe in the physical world have their origin in the spiritual world. They are taught to us as physical laws. The law of inertia says a body in motion will remain in motion unless it's acted upon by some other force. By that law, I could take a tennis ball and throw it toward Nashville, over thirty miles away, and it would travel the whole way—what an arm! This is true unless it's acted upon by another force, like gravity. Thanks to gravity, the ball won't make it across the street!

You and I have to understand there are competing forces in our lives. Most of us get mad at God and say, "I don't know why God would ..." and then we fill in what we don't like. We have a total lack of awareness that there is evil at work in the world. What's tearing the seams of our nation and our world is not a cultural clash or an ideological diversion. It's evil.

Let's imagine the spiritual world is real, and it impacts your life. (Just as we've been saying throughout this whole book!) If you'll accept those two premises, then it's in your best interest to understand how to cooperate more fully with the Spirit of God and how to resist or limit the influences of unclean spirits in your life.

Then, you need to recognize that you have spiritual influence. What you do matters.

When Jesus was in His hometown, Scripture says He could do very few miracles because of the people's unbelief. In a similar instance, Pilate condemned Jesus because he was afraid of the political pressure pushing on him. What if Pilate had the courage to say, "I believe!" Imagine if Pilate had knelt in front of Jesus and said, "I should have worshiped You." Think of the difference that would have made!

I don't know where you're in a battle or where there's a tug-of-war in your heart, but I'm quite confident there is one. If there's not, there's one in somebody you care about. Think of the difference it could make, if you were to yield to the Lordship of Jesus and unleash that spiritual authority in your life. On the other side of the equation, think of what would happen if you yielded to darkness, wickedness, immorality, ungodliness, greed, and perversion. Think of what would be unleashed in your life. You have spiritual influence!

Take Inventory

Here's a little spiritual inventory you can take:

1. Do you purposely involve yourself in spiritual things every day? Purposely, not accidentally. If the answer is yes, what does that look like for you?
2. How is the Holy Spirit involved in your daily life in a conscious, intentional, purposeful way? In what ways do you extend invitations to Him? In what ways do you behave that give Him the possibility of engaging with you more fully?
3. Are you aware of satanic or demonic influences in your

life? These aren't necessarily within you, but are there places where you realize their presence or bump against them? Maybe it's things you're watching or music or podcasts you're listening to. It may be seen in the behaviors of authorities who are over you. It may be people you're trying to lead. Perhaps you're experiencing resistance that's illogical and irrational.

4. Ask God to reveal to you if there is any place where you're engaging satanic or demonic activity. Say, "Lord, if I'm unaware of it, help me be aware!" That's a good prayer to live with in your prayer life. You want to know if you're near someone who has a contagious disease, so why wouldn't you want to be aware when you're encountering the activity of unclean spirits? You might say, "Well, I've never thought of that. I don't know how I'd recognize it. Do demons wear signs?" Becoming aware begins by getting to know the Holy Spirit. But before that, it starts with a desire—the intent to draw closer to God and gain new understanding.

Know Who to Invite into Your Life

When we talk about the Spirit of God and the angels, we want to extend frequent invitations to them, saying prayers like, "God, You're welcome in my life. Send Your angels to protect me. If there's any hurtful thing in me, I want to see it. Search my heart, God."

On the other end of the spectrum, when we talk about unclean spirits, evil spirits, and demonic spirits, we want to know how to rid ourselves from their influence. We want to do everything we can to separate ourselves from their activity. We'll talk about a set of behaviors that can help in the chapters ahead.

Do you believe in evil? I do, and I hope you'll join me. It will change the effectiveness of our faith. It will change the lives and the futures of our children and our grandchildren. We will stop delegating our futures to politicians if we accept some responsibility for ourselves. God is asking us to become a generation of overcomers. That doesn't mean just overcoming the hurts in our lives—that's the narrowest definition. We are called to be a generation that overcomes the evil that's present in our generation.

I want to pray that the Spirit of God would give us the ability to believe in Him more fully than we have before. You grow in belief like you grow in physical strength or acquire a new language. It's a progressive thing, not static. The way we knew God ten years ago is not adequate for the challenges we face today. To overcome evil, we need to know God in a new way.

LET'S PRAY

Heavenly Father, thank You for Your Word—for its truth, power, and influence. I pray that, by Your Spirit, You will give it life within me. Help me to see myself, my family, and my world

from Your vantage point. Lord, if there are places where I've been deceived or have wandered off center, I invite You to give me a revelation of myself, that I might turn to You. Lord, I don't want to share with others and then miss the opportunities You created me for. Holy Spirit, I thank You for Your presence, that You're my Teacher and my Guide. Give me a spirit of boldness. Let the fear of the Lord grow within me, and help us become a generation that overcomes evil. In Jesus' name, amen.

15 CHAPTER FIFTEEN

SPIRITUAL TERRORISM

We've spent a good amount of time talking about how to invite the Spirit of God into our lives and how to be aware of the angels God sent to help us. At the same time, we need to be equally aware of the spiritual forces of darkness arrayed against us—because they're just as certain. This is not a theoretical topic. We need to understand how to engage in that conflict.

The title for this particular chapter is "Spiritual Terrorism," and I don't intend it as a threat. One of the ways to better understand history is by studying methods of warfare. World War I was about trench warfare. Vietnam was about guerilla warfare in the jungles of Southeast Asia. For several years, we have been involved in conflicts in the desert, and those are wide open spaces, so distance matters, and covering that distance requires a different type of strategy.

In the Revolutionary War, when the farmers and the woodsmen in the colonies had to fight the British, the British assembled on the battlefield in straight lines and in bright red coats. The woodsmen from the colonies had been shooting squirrels in the forest, so they stood behind trees and shot the officers. It was an effective strategy, but it was also against the typical rules of engagement at that time.

One of the ways of understanding the changing course of history is by observing when different types of warfare have been implemented. Terrorism, as we see it today, is a change. Terrorism is about combatants on the field of conflict who don't wear uniforms and who don't identify with a nation. They're identified by an ideology. They don't acknowledge the Geneva Convention—the agreed-upon humanitarian code of conduct during conflict and war. Terrorists abide by a different moral code. Women and children are not off-limits and are instead used as weapons and shields. You may look at that practice and say, "Well, it's not right, and it's not fair." I agree, but we're naive if we don't acknowledge it.

There's a spiritual struggle taking place in the earth, and it's a conflict between good and evil. It aligns more closely in description to modern-day terrorism than the conflicts between people who agree to abide by the Geneva Convention. Evil doesn't fight fair. Its purpose is to destroy you. That's why evil is called "evil."

The Awkward Truth

We have been very vulnerable in the Church because we've heard we should love everybody. While it's true that God is love, and we have assignments to love our enemies, the Bible doesn't say we always have to be kind. Jesus wasn't always kind—He said some rather harsh things to people like the Pharisees and the money changers. Throughout Scripture, God is not always kind. He's a God of judgment just as certainly as He's a God of love, and the Church is going to have to mature a bit. We've had so much affluence and security that we've been able to cultivate a rather theoretical faith. But the world has changed, and the Church is going to have to grow with that.

This is a rather awkward truth, and saying "awkward" doesn't mean it's less significant or important. Have you ever gone to the doctor and gotten an awkward truth? The doctor says, "You're too heavy," and you reply, "No, I'm too short." I've never won that argument, but it makes perfect sense to me—at 6'5", my weight would be healthy.

Awkward truth is truth you would rather avoid. You don't want to think about it. You'd rather not dwell on it. You'd just rather move on saying, "Can't we think about something happier? That's a little awkward." Typically, the best way through awkward truth is to accept it as soon as possible, meet it head-on, and embrace it fully, completely, and totally. I would submit that's true with this particular discussion on angels, demons, and their influence on you. Awareness is key. It matters.

Identifying the Conflict

In John, chapter 10, verse 10, Jesus said, "'*The thief [Satan] comes only to steal and kill and destroy; I have come that they may have life, and have it to the full.*'"

In this verse, Jesus defined the broad parameters of our lives. We're caught in the conflict between the Kingdom of Light, which is the Kingdom of God, and the kingdom of darkness. There is not a third option. Satan and his entire kingdom have one ultimate objective: your destruction. If they can't totally destroy your life, they'll do their best to disrupt it and steal what God intended you to have. They'll try to discourage you, diminish you, limit your effectiveness, hinder you, hamper you, and torment you.

Satan's kingdom is one of torment, diminishment, and destruction. When you entertain ungodliness, immorality, wickedness, or darkness, you invite that into your life. Just as certainly, when you invite the Spirit of God into your life and you choose Jesus as Lord, you choose deliverance, restoration, forgiveness, and wholeness. Jesus told us this truth in the verse we just read—it isn't some abstract notion of a preacher. The fullest possible life for a human being is one yielded to the Lordship of Jesus of Nazareth. He won't diminish you. He won't take something from you. He won't limit you. In fact, He'll take the limits off your life.

As Christ-followers, we are engaged in a conflict. When we

choose to participate in the Kingdom of God, we become a target of the enemy. It's an awkward truth, but ignoring it won't change its reality.

So, what do we do? Remember Romans, chapter 12, and verse 21: *"Do not be overcome by evil, but overcome evil with good."*

We find multiple assignments in that short little sentence. First, don't allow evil to overcome you. Recognize it for what it is. Don't yield to it. Don't accommodate it. Don't give it greater authority.

We're also told to overcome evil. That's not a passive response like withdrawing and isolating. It's an assertive assignment: Overcome evil. It seems to me that the twenty-first century Church (and much of the twentieth century Church) chose a different path. We chose to overlook evil, and by doing so, we accommodated it. I believe we'll be held accountable if we spend our lives overlooking evil.

How do we overcome evil? Not with anger, hate, violence, or politics. Scripture tells us to overcome evil with good. God has made abundant provision for us to be overcomers, so we don't have to lead lives of fear—even though fear is stalking the streets of our nation. We're afraid to say what we think. We're afraid for our own physical health. We're afraid for our children. We're afraid for our resources. Church, we don't need to fear—we have an answer!

Pursue Righteousness

Listen to what Psalm 98, verses 1 and 2 say: *"Sing to the LORD a new song, for he has done marvelous things; his right hand and his holy arm have worked salvation for him. The LORD has made his salvation known and revealed his righteousness to the nations."*

You wouldn't need to sing a new song if your old song was perfect. But with new seasons comes the need for new songs—and we need some new songs! The world is changing, and we need to understand, in a new way, what it means to be the Church.

I intend to be part of the generation that sees the righteousness of our Lord declared to the nations. For too long, we've apologized for trying to reach the nations, saying, "Well, we don't want to appropriate another person's culture." But if a culture is destructive, diminishing, or facilitating evil in the lives of people, Jesus is always a better solution. All worldviews aren't the same. All belief systems don't have the same outcomes. There aren't many approaches to God. In John, chapter 14, verse 6, Jesus said, *"'I am the way and the truth and the life. No one comes to the Father except through me.'"* If the Church doesn't believe that statement, who will?

Our job is not to be angry or critical. Isaiah, chapter 42, verse 6 says, *"'I, the LORD, have called you in righteousness.'"* Righteousness is a big word. In the biblical sense, "righteousness" is the ability to stand in the presence of God without fear, guilt, and shame.

You see, we're all broken. Nobody wants the darkest chapters of their life projected on the big screens at church. What if we had "spiritual detectors" at our church doors like they have metal detectors at the airports? When you walked through that "spiritual detector," it would flash on the screen the dark parts of your heart. If we had those, the building would be empty—even the pastor would be outside!

Righteousness isn't about what we do—it is a gift to us, through faith in the redemptive work of Jesus Christ. When we accept Jesus as Lord of our lives, we receive the gift of righteousness so we might have the help, power, and authority of the Spirit of God as we begin to learn to lead lives that honor God. You can't accept the gift of righteousness, then give yourself to unrighteousness, and think that you will receive the benefit. You have to care about cultivating right standing with God. It needs to matter to you.

God Will Help Us!

God won't make you stop sinning, but He can give you the power to overcome it.

Isaiah, chapter 42, verse 6 continues, *"'I will take hold of your hand. I will keep you and will make you to be a covenant for the people and a light for the Gentiles.'"* I like the image of that. It's like a small child taking a parent's hand in a frightening situation. The child will find your hand, and the size difference always makes an impact upon them, as if your size is a protection. God Himself said He will "take us by the hand."

We need to have the humility to say, "God, I need Your help. *We* need Your help. I want to take Your hand." For all our experience and all we represent—it's amazing the gifts God gives us, and the things He entrusts to us—He's not like us. He spoke the world into existence. He understands the nature of the spiritual conflict we face. I don't believe God is trivial with His resources, or that He uses them unnecessarily. If He created hundreds of millions of angels to be available to us, it's because we need their assistance.

I come to the end of myself, my wisdom, and my planning on a daily basis. I tell the Lord, "I need Your help. There are things arrayed around me and standing in opposition to me that are more powerful than I'm capable of overcoming. God, help me." Day, after day, after day, I watch Him make a way. It's not always what I want—I typically want Him to totally annihilate anything that would impede or resist me. But God says, "No, that's not what we're going to do. Let Me show you the way. I will help you through today."

Be a Light

As we've discussed, the spiritual battle raging in the earth right now is not a new struggle. This is not the first time. We're not the first generation to encounter this. There have been generations where tremendous, awful, destructive forces have been unleashed on humanity. When those types of things bump into us, we tend to say, "Oh, it has to be the end of the world." Then we craft a theology that says, "Well, I'm not going to have to deal with the end of the world, so I don't have to pay any attention. Let's go back to the party." What a destructive notion!

When we see darkness increasing, we have to understand we have an assignment to be light. This is not a new thing. Acts, chapter 4, verses 1 and 2, say, *"The priests and the captain of the temple guard and the Sadducees came up to Peter and John while they were speaking to the people. They were greatly disturbed because the apostles were teaching the people, proclaiming in Jesus the resurrection of the dead."* Note that they were disturbed and angry because the disciples were talking about Jesus being raised from the dead, declaring Him to be the Son of God. The opposition hasn't changed much in 2,000 years. That story is resisted right now, all over our nation.

It continues in verses 3 and 4: *"They seized Peter and John and, because it was evening, they put them in jail until the next day. But many who heard the message believed; so the number of men who believed grew to about five thousand."*

Peter and John were put in jail because they were talking about Jesus. Are you willing to spend the night in jail so the gospel can proliferate? We've gotten a little soft. We think suffering is parking two rows further away from the sanctuary than we wanted to, not sitting in our usual seats in the sanctuary, or participating in worship songs we don't really like.

A little further in the story, Acts, chapter 14, verses 21 and 22, say, *"They preached the gospel in that city and won a large number of disciples. Then they returned to Lystra, Iconium and Antioch, strengthening the disciples and encouraging them to remain true to the faith."* This was their message to the disciples: "We must go through many hardships to enter the Kingdom of God." Why do we go through hardships? Because life is hard? No. Because there is a conflict in the earth. There are spiritual forces influencing your life today—some are for you, and some oppose you. It's time to recognize them and be a light.

Belief Versus Unbelief

In Acts, chapter 19, Paul was in the city of Ephesus, and he was having some success with the gospel message. Verses 8 and 9 say, *"Paul entered the synagogue and spoke boldly there for three months, arguing persuasively about the kingdom of God. But some of them became obstinate; they refused to believe and publicly maligned the Way."* Please note their choice: They refused to believe. When you choose against God, what you're doing—whether it's on purpose or not—is aligning yourself with the kingdom of darkness. Unbelief is not a casual thing.

When you believe God and believe His Word, and when you're faithful to God and His Word, you bring yourself into alignment with His Kingdom.

The contrast is refusing to believe. Instead of asking God for clarity as you read the Bible, you take the seat of a skeptic and say, "I just don't know if I believe that." If you find yourself in that position, know you are standing in a very dangerous place. You are willingly aligning yourself with the forces that oppose God.

In Acts, chapter 19, the disciples were in Ephesus, and many people were believing—but those who refused to believe were publicly maligning the disciples' efforts. The result? Verses 9 and 10 say Paul leaves: *"So Paul left them. He took the disciples with him and had discussions daily in the lecture hall of Tyrannus. This went on for two years, so that all the Jews and Greeks who lived in the province of Asia heard the word of the Lord."* Out of this adversity, an entire region of the world heard the gospel. This illustrates how good things can come out of difficult situations, even when people reject you.

Then, verses 11 and 12 say, *"God did extraordinary miracles through Paul, so that even handkerchiefs and aprons that had touched him were taken to the sick, and their illnesses were cured and the evil spirits left them."*

Are you willing to receive in that way? If you went into church and asked someone to pray for you, and they gave you a cloth they prayed over and asked to lay it on you, would you be content? You might think, *I know it's in the Bible, but it's weird. It's not what I want.* I understand that, but I think part of what God is awakening us to is not just how to get what we want, in the way we want it, but how to cooperate with Him.

Verses 13 through 15 continue the story:

> *Some Jews who went around driving out evil spirits tried to invoke the name of the Lord Jesus over those who were demon-possessed. They would say, "In the name of the Jesus whom Paul preaches, I command you to come out." Seven sons of Sceva, a Jewish chief priest, were doing this. One day the evil spirit answered them, "Jesus I know, and Paul I know about, but who are you?"*

It's not apparent in English, but in Greek there are two different words for the word "know." When it says, "Jesus I *know*," there is one Greek word used, and when it says, "I *know* about Paul," it's a different Greek word. In essence, it says, "Jesus I understand. I know about Paul, but I don't know you."

Verses 16 and 17 continue: *"Then the man who had the evil spirit jumped on them and overpowered them all. He gave them such a beating that they ran out of the house naked and bleeding. When this became known to the Jews and Greeks living in Ephesus, they were all seized with fear, and the name of the Lord Jesus was held in high honor."*

Note that, once again, God took something that was a disastrous failure and used it for His purposes.

Verse 18 says, *"Many of those who believed …."* Remember those words, "those who believed," because the rest of what we're about to read is something that took place in the community of believers—not among the pagans. Paul had been preaching for three months, and there was quite a community of believers. *"Many of those who believed now came and openly confessed what they had done."*

Do we have the imagination that, in the midst of those who believe, there is still the intentional cultivation of sin?

Verses 19 and 20 continue: *"A number who had practiced sorcery brought their scrolls together and burned them publicly. When they calculated the value of the scrolls, the total came to fifty thousand drachmas. In this way the word of the Lord spread widely and grew in power."*

How Acts 19 Applies to Us

The remarkable little story we just read is helpful to our circumstances right now. In verse 17, it talks about the fear of the Lord growing in the city, and that should be our primary objective. We want the respect, reverence, and awe of God to increase all over our communities. Coast to coast, border to border, congregation to congregation, school to school, university campus to university campus—let the fear of the Lord come! A reverence, respect, and sense of awe for God would be a very good thing.

Verse 18 says the believers repented. That's where change will begin—in the hearts of God's people, not with the people we disagree with. We need to stop defending our positions and begin to say to the Lord, "If there is any place in my heart, in my life, in my practice, that limits what You could or would do, help me to see it. I want to change." We desperately need some change, and it has to begin within us.

When the believers repented, they made a tremendous financial sacrifice to separate themselves from sin. It's a little hard to grasp because of the measures that are used, but it says they burned scrolls valued at 50,000 drachma. A drachma was a coin that was worth about a day's wage. The number is a little fluid, but if the value was $100 each, that means 50,000 drachmas would be worth $5 million. They didn't sell their drachmas on some online marketplace. They *destroyed* $5 million worth of goods in order to distance themselves from sin. It's an important lesson.

We see the outcome in verse 20, which says, *"In this way the word of the Lord spread widely and grew in power."* In what way? By confronting demonic strongholds through repentance and separation from the occult. That is the way for the Word of God to spread widely. We see the need for the Word of God to spread in our world today. Are we willing to submit ourselves to the leading of the Holy Spirit? Are we willing to engage in the conflict? Are we willing to yield our lives to overcome evil so the Word of God can spread widely?

This means letting go of the attitude that things would get better if the wicked people would just change. That's a popular message that works on every side of the aisle and among every group. All you have to do is identify the wicked people as those not in front of you. All around us, we see people speaking to various audiences saying polar opposite things, trying to win influence and curry favor. But with the people of God, that's not a good idea. If we'll begin to humble ourselves and say, "Lord, I'm willing to be different," God will move. He will bring salvation. He'll take things that seem to be humiliating and destructive and cause them to become powerful tools for His purposes. He'll take the most broken places in our lives—the places where our weakness can't be hidden—and His strength will be made evident and give hope to other people with those same places of brokenness and weakness. We don't have to hide our failures. God is restoring them.

LET'S PRAY

Heavenly Father, we are a people in need of healing. Lord, I don't point my finger at anyone else, but I humble myself before You and ask for Your mercy. Bring healing to my heart and my life. Give me compassion for the world we live in. Give me the discernment to recognize the truth from the false. Give me the courage to choose You with my whole heart and to lay aside anything that would diminish me. Help me turn away from any compromise I've embraced. Forgive me, Father. I turn my face to You today because You're a faithful God—a God of great mercy, a God of great strength and power, and a God who

delights in showing deliverance to His people. Help me respond to You in such a way that You would be pleased to open the windows of Heaven and rain righteousness upon me and our nation, once again. In Jesus' name, amen.

SECTION FIVE

ENGAGED AND READY

16 CHAPTER SIXTEEN

UNDERSTANDING THE UNSEEN

We so easily dismiss the unseen, imagining the forces primarily shaping our lives are things in the material world. That is almost the exact opposite of what the Bible invites us to believe.

Prior to our discovery of microscopic organisms, most of life was blamed on spiritual things. We see this in Greek and Roman mythology. Then, during the Enlightenment or the Age of Reason in the 17th and 18th centuries in Europe, "reason" was elevated above almost all other aspects of our person. That's when spiritual influences, for the most part, were dismissed. They were considered to be outdated, and that type of thinking has continued into our technological age. After all, now we have scientific investigation and rational diagnostics.

Both of those extremes—that everything is spiritual, or there is no spiritual and everything is material—leave us with an incomplete understanding. I am very grateful for science and the scientific method. I'm probably most comfortable in that world. But I also believe in the spiritual realities that influence our lives.

The Wizard of Oz presented a very fierce and intimidating scenario, until Dorothy's dog, Toto, pulled back the curtain. Once you saw what was behind that curtain, the situation became less frightening. In a similar way, spiritual things are often fierce and intimidating until we gain the insight to understand them. Books like this can help us explore those spiritual things. Instead of spending our lives looking away from them, we can benefit from the revelation and insight God offers us.

Every dark and evil character created by authors or Hollywood is only the Devil's shadow. They are poor imitations of reality. There is no battle scene from *The Lord of the Rings* that compares with the ferocity of the angelic conflict that's being waged in the earth today. Even the dreaded Borg of *Star Trek* are assimilated by the Devil and his army of demons. The masses who were slaughtered by Hitler and Stalin represent only a fraction of the lives that have been destroyed by Satan. So, when we ignore the reality of Satan and refuse to acknowledge his role, influence, and power, we're abandoning humanity, our own lives, and our families to his destructive intent.

Throughout our Bibles, men and women are urged to fight the enemy—to do battle and to wage war. We have not been placed in some sort of a spiritual amusement park and told to just have fun. I know we prefer to tell the story in that way, but a casual observation of our world would suggest otherwise. At birth, we enter the battlefield. At the time of our rebirth in Christ, we are enlisted in God's army as warriors of light. It's time to grow up.

You might be thinking, *Pastor, I don't really want to do that. I just don't want to go to Hell.* That's okay. Where you stand today is an entry point. Not wanting to go to Hell is a motivation for believing in Jesus—and that's acceptable—but as you begin to grow up in the Lord, there are responsibilities that come with being a citizen of the Kingdom of God.

Newborn babies don't have any responsibility as citizens or members of a family system. They're hungry and they cry—they want to be fed. They're dirty and uncomfortable, and they cry—they want to be changed. That's their worldview. That may be an acceptable worldview for a brand-new Christian, but if you've been a Christ-follower for forty years, and you still cry when you're hungry or need to be changed, it's time to grow up.

Abraham's nephew, Lot, learned this lesson on the evening the two angels told him to gather his family and get out of town because God intended to destroy the city where he lived. God was the impetus behind the destruction of that city. I think we could say up to that point, Lot was self-absorbed, choosing where he wanted to live based on the economic opportunities he imagined it presented. Then, God rocked his world with an angelic visit, and choosing to listen saved his family from the city's destruction.

Moses was quite satisfied being a sheep herder until the Angel of the Lord appeared to him in the flames of a burning bush, and he suddenly realized he was involved in a spiritual battle. The angel informed Moses he was being recruited to confront Pharaoh, securing the release of the Hebrew slaves.

Gideon lacked spiritual vision. He understood himself, his family, and his tribe to be insignificant, until the day the Angel of the Lord interrupted his life, sending him to battle the Midianites—the people who were plundering the whole nation of Israel. God said, "Go in the strength that you have."

Gideon countered, "It's not enough."

Then, God told him, "Hush. Move." And the Midianite army was destroyed.

We need to stop telling God what we can't do. It's time to move.

The stories could go on and on, but each of these persons fought in the power of God against forces empowered by Satan and his demons. We are the people fighting this battle in the twenty-first century. We're living in a time with conflict erupting all over the earth. It's a spiritual conflict—a war for our souls. The enemy wants to capture our affection and direct our plans. He seeks to destroy us and our families.

When you compromise and choose ungodliness and immorality, giving in to your carnal nature and those works of the flesh, you give a foothold to a spirit that intends to destroy you. He is a deceiver. He promises you pleasure and satisfaction, but his intent is your destruction.

Now, I understand some of you reading this think I'm using some very melodramatic language, and that I may be trying to frighten you into some type of fanatical faith. Let me be perfectly clear: I have no intent of frightening you. That's not my goal. Recognizing spiritual conflict is not the realm of fanatics unless you perceive Jesus and His disciples to be fanatics. So, let's take a few minutes and try to gain some more understanding about the unseen world.

God's Invisible Qualities

Romans, chapter 1, verse 20 says, *"For since the creation of the world God's invisible qualities—his eternal power and divine nature—have been clearly seen, being understood from what has been made, so that people are without excuse."*

God has qualities that are invisible to us. Just because we can't see those qualities doesn't mean they don't exist. You and I interact with our world through five senses, but those five senses do not define reality. Our senses have limits. Dogs have a more acute sense of hearing than humans. Other animals have visual abilities that we don't have—you've heard about "an eagle eye." It's a rational, logical conclusion to realize our five senses should not define reality—if they did, there would be no such thing as a virus because you can't see it with your eyes. But even if you can't see the virus itself physically, you can see the impact of it and its influence.

In a similar way, the Bible tells us God has qualities that are invisible to our physical senses. God's creation serves as a canvas, giving us insight on God's eternal power and His divine nature. Creation makes God accessible to us in a way that we can perceive and understand Him with our senses to such an extent that, if you see and experience creation and still deny God, you are without excuse (see Romans 1:20).

The Bible opens by presenting God to us as the Creator. We're perverse when we refuse to acknowledge Him as Creator or say the world around us "just happened," even though that's an illogical conclusion. It's far more probable that this book "just happened" to come together—trees toppled in the woods, rain fell and broke the wood down, the cellulose reassembled itself into thin sheets. There were all sorts of leaves and creatures in the woods with different colors, and when they died, the pigment from the leaves and from their bodies leached together through the soil and found its way to those sheets of cellulose that had formed from the decaying trees and arranged themselves on a page in an orderly fashion for you to read.

If you think I'm being too dramatic, that's what current theories preach: Living organisms came out of the primordial ooze, and all the proteins happened to align themselves perfectly. It's much easier to believe this book happened than you just happened.

There is a Creator.

How did He do it? I don't know.

Was it a big bang, a little bang, lots of bang? I don't know.

We don't have full disclosure on how creation happened. We operate on a need-to-know basis. If you don't like that reality, you can talk to the Boss next time you see Him. In the meantime, let's humble ourselves and take Him at His Word.

Hebrews, chapter 11, verse 3 says, *"By faith we understand that the universe was formed at God's command ...."*

It would be an interesting exercise to write down what you understand by faith. It's easy to tell me what you understand by study. What do you understand about English, from all of your years in school? What do you understand about mathematics? Those are all legitimate subjects, but I'm more interested in knowing what you understand by faith. How does your faith impact your life? How does it influence your values? How does it change your calendar? How does it affect your resources and how you manage them?

By Faith

Hebrews, chapter 11, verse 3 continues, "... *so that what is seen was not made out of what was visible."*

This verse shows us that the material, physical world we see was given order and shape from the spiritual world—a place we aren't currently able to perceive as well as we would like. One day we will. Here is the important thing to recognize: We don't lack the ability to "sense" what's going on in the spiritual world—we just haven't learned how to engage it more fully. It's like buying a subscription to a cable or streaming service—if you pay a higher fee, you'll gain more access. In a similar way, if you invest in learning about spiritual things, you will gain abilities and insights beyond what you currently know.

The Bible says that now we see as if we're looking through glass, darkly, as if the mirror is fogged over—but the day is coming when we will see clearly. It says, now we know in part, but there's a day ahead of us when we will know fully (see 1 Corinthians 13:12). Don't let your limited perceptions be the primary determiner for how you interact in the world. Begin to see the world from a God-perspective. To understand the seen, we first have to understand the unseen.

Unholy spirits, unclean spirits, or demonic spirits—they're all synonymous terms—are prevalent throughout the story of Scripture. Earlier, we discussed how Jesus's ministry began with His interaction with a demonized man in a synagogue. We see the same type of interactions happening all through the Gospels and into Acts, when the Church begins.

Paul Addresses an Unclean Spirit

In Acts, chapter 16, verse 16, we find Paul in Philippi, going to the place of prayer, and he is met by a female slave who had a spirit by which she predicted the future. It was an unclean spirit.

One of the things we have learned together is that some of the unclean spirits have understanding and awareness we don't have. They recognized Jesus long before the disciples or anyone else did. In this case, there was an unclean spirit that had enough awareness of what was ahead, it helped this young girl earn a great deal of money for her owners by fortune telling.

Verse 17 tells us, *"She followed Paul and the rest of us, shouting, 'These men are servants of the Most High God, who are telling you the way to be saved.'"* What she said happened to be true. She knew something about Paul and his entourage the other people in the city didn't know. It was a spiritual understanding. So, there is insight and understanding in the spiritual world that is different from the understanding we have. However, unclean spirits don't understand everything. They would have never influenced people to crucify Jesus if they understood the purpose of the cross. It's good to know the Devil is not as smart as God, but we have to acknowledge that these demonic spirits have some insight and understanding.

The girl kept yelling, "These men are the servants of the Most High God!" How awkward would that be? Imagine going to the mall or the grocery store and having somebody follow you around, shouting that at the top of their lungs. It had to be uncomfortable, and she kept it up for many days. Verse 18 says, *"Finally Paul became so annoyed that he turned around and said to the spirit, 'In the name of Jesus Christ I command you to come out of her!' At that moment the spirit left her."*

Note that Paul addressed the spirit, not the girl. The encounter with an unclean and unholy spirit is not a power encounter. You don't need to power up to defeat the enemy. It's a truth encounter. It's about understanding the authority you have in Christ and the lack of authority that spirit has. When Paul said, "In the name of Jesus, you come out of her," the spirit left.

Then, Paul had a new issue to deal with. Verses 19 to 21 say, *"When her owners realized that their hope of making money was gone, they seized Paul and Silas and dragged them into the marketplace to face the authorities. They brought them before the magistrates and said, 'These men are Jews, and are throwing our city into an uproar by advocating customs unlawful for us Romans to accept or practice.'"*

That's not true. The girl's owners were lying. They were simply angry because they lost an opportunity for economic gain.

I've read this passage many times, and I have often wondered why Paul tolerated the girl for several days. Why didn't he address the spirit on his first encounter? The complete answer is not there, so we're left to some conjecture or opinion. At this point in Paul's journey, he'd experienced riots in several places. I think he understood there were going to be repercussions if he addressed the spirit.

I think you and I understand that if we take a position for the truth, and we push it into the public arena, there could be repercussions. That's why you don't do it frivolously or recklessly. But when you feel like God has put the opportunity in front of you, you do what must be done. I typically feel like God puts those opportunities in front of me until they're almost unavoidable.

Several years ago, there were some things happening in our community that were causing concern, but I had not been paying much attention. I had been busy and had a full calendar, and when people asked what I thought about the situation, I told them, "I think it's not my problem." It happened frequently enough, I finally stopped one day and said, "Lord, if You want me to do something about that situation, I need You to open a door." It was in the beginning of the day, and before noon, somebody I didn't know called me and said, "I was scheduled to speak to the county commission tonight, and I really felt prompted that you should take that time slot." I said, "Lord, I didn't really mean it when I said that this morning!" I understood my assignment wasn't an easy one, and indeed, it did not bring a parade to my door or great affirmation—but I did what the Lord told me to do.

We Can Overcome Evil

If we're going to overcome evil, we can't do it from a totally silent, camouflaged position. We need to have the courage to confront it. In the story we just discussed about the slave girl, I think Paul understood that even though the girl needed to be delivered from the evil spirit, that action would cause a great deal of consternation in the community. In that city, a portion of Satan's kingdom had been exposed and defeated, and the unclean, unholy spirits in that city hated it and the individual who took a role in it. So, whatever lying, deceptive influence they had, and whatever way they could influence the political system, they did so.

The city's response was illogical in its magnitude. They didn't care about a slave girl. They probably could have dragged her outside the city and taken her life, and nobody would have cared. It's a disproportionate response, and the only way I know to understand the larger story is in terms of spiritual things. Satan's kingdom was enraged, and it manifested itself in that city.

Spiritual forces are real. We're going to have to have the courage to stand up. Evil will not turn loose just because we wish it would. We don't have to be angry or belligerent, but we do need to take action.

We need to be willing to fast, pray, and humble ourselves.

We need to get rid of the compromise in our lives.

We need to repent of our sins, renounce them by choosing to follow a new path, and release them to God, trusting that He has forgiven us fully and completely.

We need to be willing to invite the Spirit of God into our own hearts.

That's the momentum for the changes we need.

Adjust Your Focus

So, how do we build our awareness of spiritual things? It has a lot to do with where you focus. You pay attention to the things that matter to you. If you bought a new car, you may think you purchased something unique—until you drive it home and suddenly recognize dozens of cars just like it on the road with you. If you're a hunter, you can drive down the street and you see all the wildlife. If you're a great baker, you can walk into a kitchen and immediately assess whether the person who uses that kitchen is a good baker or not. If you're a parent, you can hear 100 children cry and recognize yours. So, spiritual awareness has to do with cultivating a focus. You need to care about it.

Second Corinthians, chapter 4, verse 18 tells us, *"So we fix our eyes not on what is seen, but on what is unseen, since what is seen is temporary, but what is unseen is eternal."*

How do you look at what you cannot see? We need a different perspective. Our valuation system needs to be different from the secular culture's. If you think your future is secured by Wall

Street, you're not really behaving any differently than the rest of the world. If you believe your future is secured by the contacts you have in the world, how are you different from the people who don't believe in God and who do not have Jesus as Lord of their lives? There should be a different set of criteria for us. Again, we don't need to be removed from the world. It's not wrong to be involved with what's happening on Wall Street. I just think we need to understand it can't secure our future.

Strengthen the Inner Man

Ephesians, chapter 3, verse 16 says, *"I pray that out of his glorious riches he may strengthen you with power through his Spirit in your inner being."* That's not the way I would have written the prayer. My first thought would be to pray that you'd have strength like Samson. Forget the inner man—I want some serious muscle power! Our "inner man being renewed" is a more persistent theme in Scripture than we may imagine. I'm not sure we've held the value of being strengthened in our inner man, but that was Paul's prayer for the church at Ephesus, and for us.

Peter, the fisherman Jesus recruited, said to not let your imagination of beauty or personal worth be merely external. Instead, 1 Peter, chapter 3, verse 4 says, *"But it should be the hidden person of the heart, with the imperishable quality of a gentle and quiet spirit, which is precious in the sight of God"* (NASB®). When you find something that the Bible says is precious in the sight of God, cultivate that. Do everything in your power to let it flourish in you. If you're displaying something that contrasts or diminishes that, you need to cultivate less of that and more of what is precious in God's sight.

This scripture tells us a gentle and quiet spirit is imperishable. It will never diminish. That means it's an investment. It's worth meditating on. What would a gentle and quiet spirit look like for you? It doesn't mean you're always quiet; it doesn't mean you don't have an opinion. I'll leave that for you to think about.

We see another discussion about the inner and outer man in Colossians, chapter 3, verses 9 and 10: *"Do not lie to each other, since you have taken off your old self with its practices and have put on the new self, which is being renewed in knowledge in the image of its Creator."*

Paul is talking to the church in Colossae about putting off an old self, with its set of behaviors and practices, so the inner man can be renewed. We find a little more definition around that by going to Galatians and reading the list of the works of the flesh (our old nature):

> *The acts of the flesh are obvious: sexual immorality, impurity and debauchery; idolatry and witchcraft; hatred, discord, jealousy, fits of rage, selfish ambition, dissensions, factions and envy; drunkenness, orgies, and the like. I warn you, as I did before, that those who live like this will not inherit the kingdom of God.*
>
> GALATIANS 5:19-21

This is a good sampling of the types of things you want to stop doing—they lead to destruction.

Then, Paul contrasts those behaviors by looking at the fruit of the Spirit in verses 22 and 23: *"But the fruit of the Spirit is love, joy, peace, forbearance, kindness, goodness, faithfulness, gentleness and self-control. Against such things there is no law."* These are the behaviors you want to cultivate—they will lead to God's blessings and good things in your life. It's not easy, and it's not intuitive. If you don't cultivate it, the fruit won't be there—because it's about strengthening your character, and that takes diligence, intentionality, and practice.

Now is a good time to remind you that 2 Corinthians, chapter 4, verse 17, says that our troubles—our light and momentary afflictions—produce eternal glory. Are you ready for that idea? Afflictions actually create opportunities for us, even though it doesn't feel that way when we're in the midst of them.

Recognize What's Temporary and What's Eternal

Scripture tells us not to focus on the things we see, but we often do. That's what we get mad and anxious about. It's what frightens and frustrates us. We focus on the traffic. Why does it take so long to drive across town? Because the town needs us to pray more. So, stop moaning about the traffic, and start praying! The Devil might clear the lanes to shut you up! Turn off the radio in your car and begin to pray in the Spirit. Thank God for renewal in your community, for an outpouring of His Spirit, and that the fear of the Lord will preside over the nearby schools and college campuses. Every time you drive through a school zone, pray for the school: "Lord, pour out Your Spirit on those students."

We need to learn to stop focusing on our temporary troubles and instead bring our attention to the Kingdom of God. Let's become more invested in the eternal and turn loose of the temporary. Afterall, you have rewards that are being stored up from an unseen source. Matthew, chapter 6, verse 6 says, *"'But when you pray, go into your room, close the door and pray to your Father, who is unseen. Then your Father, who sees what is done in secret, will reward you.'"*

The Bible very clearly teaches us the unseen world can see you. Remember that.

The Spiritual Realm Impacts the Physical Realm

Throughout the Bible, we find outcomes in the visible, physical realm that were clearly driven by unseen things in the spiritual realm. One example is in Matthew, chapter 17, when the disciples needed to pay the temple tax. Jesus gave Peter some specific instructions in verse 27: *"'But so that we may not cause offense, go to the lake and throw out your line. Take the first fish you catch; open its mouth and you will find a four-drachma coin. Take it and give it to them for my tax and yours.'"* I don't think Peter caught many fish with money in its mouth. But Jesus clearly had an insight and awareness—an impact on the physical realm that began in a spiritual place.

We see a different context in Mark, chapter 5, where we find a story of a woman who was sick and had pursued every medical avenue available. Verses 27 and 28 say, *"When she heard about Jesus, she came up behind him in the crowd and touched his cloak, because she thought, 'If I just touch his clothes, I will be healed.'"* That was her conviction. By faith, she understood something. By just touching His clothes, she was healed immediately, her bleeding stopped, and she felt in her body that she had been freed from her suffering.

In the scene, Jesus was in a large crowd with many people jostling against Him. In fact, when Jesus stopped and asked, "Who touched Me?" The disciples said, "Are You kidding? You're elbowing Your way through a crowd." Jesus said, "No, somebody touched Me in a different way. Who was that?" I think Jesus knew precisely who it was, but He was giving the woman an opportunity to come to Him. Verses 33 and 34 say, *"Then the woman, knowing what had happened to her, came and fell at his feet and, trembling with fear, told him the whole truth. He said to her, 'Daughter, your faith has healed you. Go in peace and be freed from your suffering.'"*

Again, we find unseen influences creating some very tangible outcomes—in this case, a miraculous healing. It doesn't mean every time you pray, you'll get the outcome you think you want. Oftentimes, we pray from a very limited perspective, and we don't have the discernment or the wisdom to know the outcome we need. Think of what your life would be like if every prayer you ever prayed was answered in the affirmative. We would be train wrecks! Don't you know that the angels smile at some of our prayers?

Use Your Words for Good

Your words have spiritual authority—it's a biblical principle. You can use your words for good or for evil. There have been words that have been spoken to you that have stayed with you over long periods of time. That's true when it comes to negative words, and I assure you, it's equally true of positive ones.

A proclamation is when we take what God's Word says about us, and we agree with it, making it a personal declaration. When we do this, we align our lives with God's Truth. It's a powerful way to speak the truth of Scripture over your life. I brought you two proclamations, and I gave you the scriptures I used to build them. The scripture shows the authority from which these statements were derived.

The first one is about God's protection because we need to know God is our Protector. I didn't change the scriptures, but if I were saying these aloud to myself, I would take the pronouns and make them personal, saying, "One thousand may fall at *my* side and ten thousand at *my* left hand, but it won't come near *me*." I don't want Scripture to be theoretical. I want it to be true in my life. Take the time now to read the following aloud.

Proclamation of God's Protection

I rejoice in the protection of Almighty God over my life. I am the Lord's servant. I rest in the completeness of His strength and care. No weapon formed against me will prevail. I will refute every tongue that rises against me. This is my heritage as a servant of the Lord. A thousand may fall at my side, but destruction will not overwhelm me. I have made the Most High my dwelling place. God is my refuge and my security. No harm will befall me. No disaster will overtake me. God has commanded His angels to watch over my life. My life and my future are secure through the strength of my Lord and my Redeemer.

"No weapon forged against you will prevail, and you will refute every tongue that accuses you. This is the heritage of the servants of the LORD, and this is their vindication from me," declares the LORD.

ISAIAH 54:17

A thousand may fall at your side, ten thousand at your right hand, but it will not come near you. You will only observe with your eyes and see the punishment of the wicked. If you say, "The LORD is my refuge," and you make the Most High your dwelling, no harm will overtake you, no disaster will come near your tent. For he will command his angels concerning you to guard you in all your ways.

PSALM 91:7-11

This next proclamation can help strengthen you when you are discouraged or tempted to lose heart. Read it aloud now.

Proclamation of Hope and Restoration

I put on the garment of praise and hope. I choose the joy of the Lord as my strength. I lay aside the spirit of heaviness and raise my voice in praise of the Living God. May my eyes be open to the provision of God and my ears attentive to the sound of His deliverance. Holy Spirit, help me. In You I find power and revelation. God has restored my broken heart and set my feet on a path of victory. I have hope for today and the strength to complete the course You have chosen for me. Let the people of God arise triumphant, and may the name of Jesus be lifted up throughout the earth. In Jesus' name, amen.

The LORD is close to the brokenhearted and saves those who are crushed in spirit. The righteous person may have many troubles, but the LORD delivers him from them all.

PSALM 34:18-19

The Spirit of the Sovereign LORD is on me, because the LORD has anointed me to proclaim good news to the poor. He has sent me to bind up the brokenhearted, to proclaim freedom for the captives and release from darkness for the prisoners, to proclaim the year of the LORD's favor and the day of vengeance of our God, to comfort all who mourn, and provide for those who grieve in Zion—to bestow on them a crown of beauty instead of ashes, the oil of joy instead of mourning, and a garment of praise instead of a spirit of despair. They will be called oaks of righteousness, a planting of the LORD for the display of his splendor.

ISAIAH 61:1-3

17 CHAPTER SEVENTEEN

THE NEED FOR DISCERNMENT

Discernment is a big religious word that has to do with your awareness of angels, demons, and spiritual things. Spiritual discernment is one of the gifts that comes with the Spirit of God living within you, as a Christ-follower. If you have little awareness of spiritual things, that means you're receiving little input from the Spirit of God. That's a dangerous way to live in the world today. We want to cultivate discernment, but to do that, we need to have a better understanding of what it is.

Second Kings paints a picture between someone who is spiritually aware alongside someone who is oblivious. The city the prophet Elisha was staying in was surrounded by a foreign army, and Elisha prays for his servant in 2 Kings, chapter 6, verse 17: *"'Open his eyes, LORD, so that he may see.' Then the LORD opened the servant's eyes, and he looked and saw the hills full of horses and chariots of fire all around Elisha."* In the context, it seems that Elisha was aware the horses and chariots were there the entire time, but his servant was oblivious to them.

I want to put this idea on the table: It's possible to be totally unaware of what God is doing while you're standing next to someone who has an awareness. Why would you want to be the unaware person? It's in our best interest to make whatever changes we need to make and adjust whatever course corrections are available to us. We want to ask for any gifts the Lord has available to us, so we can be as spiritually aware as possible. This means we need to give the Spirit of the Lord permission to look at our lives. Then, we need to be willing to change those areas that need adjusting, purifying ourselves so we can hear Him more fully.

Snapshots of Spiritual Activity Around Jesus

I want to present a series of snapshots, or momentary glimpses, of Jesus and His Church. What I want you to notice is the spiritual activity happening around Jesus.

When Jesus was baptized, the Holy Spirit, in the form of a dove, descended upon Him in Matthew, chapter 3. Verse 17 says, *"And a voice from heaven said, 'This is my Son, whom I love; with him I am well pleased.'"* In this snapshot, we have God the Father, God the Son, and God the Holy Spirit together at Jesus' baptism. Then, Jesus goes away from the Jordan River and into the wilderness for forty days.

In Matthew, chapter 4, after forty days of fasting and praying, Jesus is tempted by Satan. We find the last of those temptations here:

> *Again, the devil took him to a very high mountain and showed him all the kingdoms of the world and their splendor. "All this I will give you," he said, "if you will bow down and worship me." Jesus said to him, "Away from me, Satan! For it is written: 'Worship the Lord your God, and serve him only.'"*
>
> MATTHEW 4:8-10

When you're trying to figure out your life, decisions, pressures, and problems, is there a place in that equation where you consider the involvement of Satan and his kingdom? It's very clear Jesus believed in him. Verse 11 says, "*Then the devil left him, and angels came and attended him.*" In this one little screenshot, you have Satan himself tempting the incarnate Son of God. Then, after Jesus resisted temptation, God sent the angels to serve Him. If you don't believe in the Devil, and you don't believe in angels, you're going to miss the Jesus-story completely.

Let's push a little further, using two different passages centered on Jesus' crucifixion.

First Corinthians, chapter 2, verse 7 says, "*No, we declare God's wisdom, a mystery that has been hidden and that God destined for our glory before time began.*" People are often frustrated because they don't understand as fully as they would like, or they don't have the insight as completely as they would prefer. But God doesn't give us total access. Part of the nature of our relationship with Him is He invites us to seek, pursue, and actually care about Him.

If you are world-class at something—it may be a hobby, passion, interest, parenting, or something else—you've cared enough about it to learn, study, refine your responses, and correct your mistakes. It's a living, dynamic thing that you have focused a great deal of time, energy, attention, and resources upon. The Creator of all things deserves the same kind of intentionality from us.

Paul told the church of Corinth that the power behind Jesus' crucifixion was the rulers of this age. "Rulers" is plural, and I don't believe Paul was talking about earthly rulers—like Caesar, Pilate, or Caiaphas. A spiritual attack took place on Golgotha that day, with spiritual forces of darkness orchestrating Jesus' execution. If they had understood God's wisdom, they would never have done it—that's why you know it's not earthly rulers. Jesus' crucifixion didn't cost Pilate, and it didn't disrupt Caesar's polling numbers. But it did totally disrupt the kingdom of darkness. Through the cross—His death, burial, and resurrection—Jesus won an eternal, complete, irreversible defeat over those unclean spirits. If they had understood the ramifications, they would have never done it.

The next passage to consider is Matthew, chapter 27, where we find the physical scene of Jesus on the cross. Jesus cried out in a loud voice and gave up His spirit, and at that moment, God tore the curtain of the Temple in two, from top to bottom. The earth shook, the rocks split, the tombs broke open, and the bodies of many holy people who had died were raised to life. They came out of the tombs, and after Jesus' resurrection, they went into the Holy City and appeared to many people.

It's an amazing snapshot to behold. In the moment of seeming triumph for the kingdom of darkness, when Jesus says, *"My God, My God, why have You forsaken Me?"* (Matthew 27:46) and He gives up His spirit, God demonstrates His power and gives us some hints of His purposes and plans.

In that day, only the high priests could go into the Holy of Holies, a sectioned off place in the Temple where the Spirit of God was said to dwell in the midst of His people. They entered through the curtain only once a year and only then with the blood of a lamb. When Jesus died, that place was made spiritually accessible to everybody. God tore open the curtain that separated the Holy of Holies, from top to bottom. The tombs opened and many dead people came to life again, but the kingdom of darkness still didn't stop pursuing its evil objectives. It's another example of the spiritual forces of darkness and the power of God at work simultaneously.

Many of us have read the Bible all our lives, but we still debate whether or not we believe in Satan, his kingdom, or unclean spirits, or whether God does miracles. The truth is we have no story unless we understand it in the context of that spiritual conflict. We tend to think, *If God is moving and doing supernatural things, surely there wouldn't be any opposition, pushback, difficulty, or confusion.* But when we read the story of the Bible, in the midst of these tremendous breakthroughs, miracles, and victories, we see satanic opposition happening, too. So, if we're going to see a move of the Spirit of God in this season, I would submit to you, it's only logical that there's going to be opposition. And it's not going to be theoretical. It's going to bump into you.

I'll give you one more example in Ephesians, chapter 1, where we find a snapshot of Jesus' exalted and triumphant Church and God's power, which verses 19 and 20 describe as, "*... his incomparably great power for us who believe. That power is the same as the mighty strength he exerted when he raised Christ from the dead and seated him at his right hand in the heavenly realms.*"

The greatest description of the power of God available to Paul, when he's writing to the church at Ephesus, was the power displayed at Jesus' crucifixion and resurrection—the most difficult season of Jesus' earthly life. When Jesus was in Gethsemane, He prayed, "God, I don't want to do this." Then, He turned to His friends and said, "Before the sun comes up, you're all going to abandon Me." There was tremendous stress in His life, yet out of that adversity, God put Jesus above every expression of spiritual darkness that sought to destroy Him. We see this in verse 21, which describes Jesus' position as *"far above all rule and authority, power and dominion, and every name that is invoked, not only in the present age but also in the one to come."*

In Philippians, chapter 2, verses 9 and 10, Paul wrote to the church to tell them that after the crucifixion, *"God exalted [Jesus] to the highest place and gave him the name that is above every name, that at the name of Jesus every knee should bow, in heaven and on earth and under the earth."* Every realm of existence, every title that can be given—not only in the present age but in the one to come—God placed all things under Jesus' feet and appointed Him to be head over everything, including the Church, which is His Body.

These verses portray of the Kingdom of God and the kingdom of darkness. They celebrate the power of God's strength. They say the power that's at work within us today has value in the present age and in the age to come.

What Can We Do?

We need discernment. We need to be aware of the angels. We need a better understanding of the spiritual forces of darkness arrayed against us, or we'll think we're dealing with a people problem, an institutional problem, a political problem, a medical problem, or some other kind of problem. We'll be completely oblivious to the root cause.

There has to be a difference between the people of God and

the people who don't know Him—and the difference has to extend further than where we sit for a few minutes on the weekend, the holidays we celebrate, or the moral code we keep. That first-century Jewish audience was all-in on religious rules and holidays, but they lacked the discernment to recognize the Messiah. We don't want to be in that group of people. Lord, give us discernment.

We need to have the courage to invite the Spirit of God into our lives. Let's stop the sloppiness and stop telling God what we won't do before we'll cooperate. I have a feeling that if one of us were stranded in a warzone tonight and somebody had three things we needed to do to get out, we'd work hard to accomplish those tasks. If they said, "You need to eat a piece of pita bread," you probably wouldn't respond, "Well, I don't really like pita." I bet you'd be eating it as quickly as possible! We haven't been desperate enough!

But how do you cultivate discernment? How do you begin to be aware of spiritual things? How do you raise your threshold? How do you become a better listener? How do you learn to have eyes of faith?

A good place to start is by asking the Lord to help you see the places where you're too connected to this present world order. One way to sort out where your heart's invested is by honestly reflecting on what brings you excitement and joy. Don't give your church answer. We all would say "Jesus." But in the quiet places of your life, what gives you excitement and joy? If the answer isn't immediately apparent, another thing to consider is this: What causes you great frustration if you think it's going to be delayed or withheld? Talk about those things with the Lord. Ask Him to show you their proper place in your life.

God made His creation for all of us, but this present world order isn't going to secure our futures. Following the world's logic won't give our children success in eternity or bring them true contentment. Those things come from the Kingdom of God. If we're going to elevate our discernment—our ability to recognize the spiritual things unfolding around us—we'll need to disassemble some of the connection points we've established with the world and our ideas of what makes us successful.

Our Struggle Is Not Against People

Ephesians, chapter 6, verse 12 says, *"For our struggle is not against flesh and blood, but against the rulers, against the authorities, against the powers of this dark world and against the spiritual forces of evil in the heavenly realms."*

If those words weren't printed in the Bible, I would not have that perspective, because it feels like most of the time the struggles in my life have to do with people. Does it feel like that to you?

The primary arena of conflict is your person: your mind, your emotions, and sometimes your body. We've looked at some examples of where unclean spirits affected people physically.

But what about where they've affected their emotional or mental state? We have this mistaken idea that we're just too sophisticated for evil. We have medicine and psychology—I advocate for both—but they don't change the reality of the spiritual conflict in the earth, and they don't hold solutions for all the problems we have.

We need to live with a heightened awareness. This doesn't mean you have to be afraid. Instead, it's a time to realize you have been given a tremendous victory.

We need to know who we are in Christ and how to put on the armor of God that's been provided to us. We see a list of armor available to us in Ephesians:

> *Therefore put on the full armor of God, so that when the day of evil comes, you may be able to stand your ground, and after you have done everything, to stand. Stand firm then, with the belt of truth buckled around your waist, with the breastplate of righteousness in place, and with your feet fitted with the readiness that comes from the gospel of peace. In addition to all this, take up the shield of faith, with which you can extinguish all the flaming arrows of the evil one. Take the helmet of salvation and the sword of the Spirit, which is the word of God.*
>
> EPHESIANS 6:13-17

We need to understand the authority of the blood of Jesus and the power of Jesus' name. We've been entrusted with both. A powerful way to remember what's true is by reading this Blood of Jesus Proclamation aloud:

Through the blood of Jesus, I am redeemed out of the hand of the Devil. Through the blood of Jesus, all my sins are forgiven. The blood of Jesus Christ, God's Son, continually cleanses me from all sin. Through the blood of Jesus, I am sanctified, made holy, set apart to God. Through the blood of Jesus, I am justified and made righteous, just as if I'd never sinned. My body is a temple of the Holy Spirit, redeemed and cleansed by the blood of Jesus. Therefore, Satan has no place in me and no power over me, through the blood of Jesus. Amen.

We also need to read our Bibles so we can understand God's perspective, what we need to yield to, and what we do not. Ignoring the facts and the tools that have been given to us doesn't remove us from the arena. It just makes us highly vulnerable.

Harassing Spirits

In the book of Luke, Jesus speaks about an unclean spirit that inhabits a human being:

> *"When an impure spirit comes out of a person, it goes through arid places seeking rest and does not find it. Then it says, 'I will return to the house I left.' When it arrives, it finds the house swept clean and put in order. Then it goes*

and takes seven other spirits more wicked than itself, and they go in and live there. And the final condition of that person is worse than the first."

LUKE 11:24-26

Unclean spirits harass people. They won't knock on your door and say, "I'm making a call for Unholy Spirits 'R Us. You've been gaining a little too much momentum with that daily Bible reading stuff, and you've gone to church three weeks in a row without even complaining about where you parked. You smiled at three people while you waited in the parking lot after church, so I'm here to knock you off your game." That's not how it happens. In the midst of your life—in your business and your assignments—something will disrupt your emotional or mental state, and you'll be angry. You may ignore it the first two or three times it knocks on your door. You might be focused enough, or busy enough, or rested enough, or insulated enough you don't yield. But if you don't recognize there's a battle taking place in your life, evil is unrelenting. That's why it's evil. Evil will take advantage of you at your most vulnerable points. Evil doesn't play fair.

So, the goal is to minimize those points of vulnerability.

Live with greater awareness.

Pray.

Offer praise and thanksgiving.

Keep short accounts. You can't afford unforgiveness or to be sloppy with your emotions—there's a conflict going on!

Don't be casual with what you watch, think about, and listen to. Don't create entry points for unclean spirits to harass you.

Don't tolerate thoughts that are ungodly. Those thoughts come to all of us, and I'm not just talking about immoral thoughts. It seems discontentment is far more destructive in this season than immorality. We're the most blessed society in history, but we are discontent. We tear down our statues, hate one another, and can't have a civil discourse. We're aware of all our problems, shortcomings, and failures—and there's a plethora of them—but we dismiss all our blessings. It's a spiritual battle. Discontentment (or a lack of contentment) reminds you of what you don't have, or how somebody looked at you, or what somebody didn't say, or what you think you're entitled to. When those thoughts come into your mind, recognize it as an unclean spirit that has come to torment you. If you give it a place, it will gain authority, and you don't want that. Instead, address it and say, "Discontentment, you are not welcome here. I am blessed!"

It's Time to Prepare!

God has been shaking the earth, and I believe He's trying to get our attention. Pay attention. Listen. Get out your Bible. Begin to talk to Him and the other fine people who are listening to Him.

There are assignments coming!

Second Chronicles, chapter 16, verse 9 says, *"For the eyes of the LORD roam throughout the earth, so that He may strongly support those whose heart is completely His"* (NASB®). He doesn't want to give us a participation trophy—He has an assignment for us! He is looking for somebody who can withstand the temptations; somebody who can walk through those difficult places; someone who has the courage to say, "I believe God can deliver and will deliver."

So, how do we prepare? I'll give you three ideas that we'll expand upon as we go forward.

1. Repent and believe. Repentance opens the door to belief. It's not the pagans who need to repent; it's the believers. Until you have fully yielded your heart to repentance, discernment will be awkward for you. Are you reluctant to be around people who you think have discernment? Do you have to shape your story to make it more palatable? Do you wear a face for one place and another face for others? Repent and believe.
2. Start to develop your listening skills. Jesus said, "My sheep know My voice." The most consistent characteristic of the people of God, from Genesis to Revelation, is they listen to Him. Develop your listening skills.
3. Make no provision for the flesh. The Bible's prescription for our carnal nature is to crucify it. Don't entertain

it, don't excuse it, and don't justify it. Don't make any provision for it.

God has an assignment for you of tremendous significance. The darkness in our earth is unprecedented, and we need recognize it and bring God's light. We need it in our schools, in our offices, in our communities, and across our nation.

LET'S PRAY

Heavenly Father, You delight in showing mercy. Through Your compassion and mercy, I have been delivered out of the kingdom of darkness. Give me an understanding heart, so I might know You more fully. Give me boldness to stand for Your truth. Give me discernment, that I might see as You see. Deliver me from evil. May Your Kingdom come and Your will be done on Earth as it is in Heaven. In Jesus' name, amen.

18 CHAPTER EIGHTEEN

AN EXIT STRATEGY

Remember, we're not going to out-think, out-organize, or overpower evil with our numbers. We've seen the folly of this approach, thinking evil will play nice. We think if we don't talk about evil, or if we can make a treaty with it, evil will treat us fairly. But the nature of evil is that it doesn't play fair. That's why we call it "evil."

We've spent quite a bit of time discussing good, evil, and the spiritual forces attached to each. We've talked about how to invite the Spirit of God into our lives and how to cultivate an awareness of what God is doing in the earth, so we become more aware of the good than we are of the evil. Those are essential practices.

What we need next is an exit strategy for evil. How do you

diminish the influence of evil in your life? You need a biblical blueprint, otherwise you'll create solutions based on your intellect, and the outcome will be just as devastating as what we see in the world around us. We need the wisdom of God.

To get started, here are some fundamentals you need to know:

First, when we talk about engaging with evil and recognizing it exists, understand it is fundamentally a truth encounter, not a power encounter. We are no match for the Devil. In fact, the Bible reminds us our heroes of the faith all struggled because of his plots and schemes. Think of Abraham and Ishmael. Moses the murderer. David the adulterer. Paul the angry, violent man. Peter, the one who denied the Lord. Nobody gets through without challenges.

We are not more powerful than the Devil, but through our faith in Jesus, we have access to the One who is. The basis of our freedom, the imagination that we can be free, is about God's Truth. "Love the truth," the Bible says. "Buy the truth, and don't sell it" (see Proverbs 23:23). There is nothing more valuable than God's Truth. Yield to God's Truth. Freedom is found on the pathway defined by God's Truth. It's why reading your Bible is so essential. Knowing the truth will help you recognize and address the lies of the enemy.

Second, I want to invite you to be aware but not afraid. Sometimes when we talk about unclean spirits, unholy spirits, demonic spirits, and fallen angels, there's a creeping sense of fear. That's not the objective of this conversation. You simply need to be aware so you can understand what gives evil access to your life and how to find freedom when that access has been granted. This is not a point of fear—it's just a reality.

I don't know whether it's true or not, but I read that the Christian reformer, Martin Luther, woke up one night to find the Devil standing at the foot of his bed. Luther said, "Oh, it's just you," and he rolled over and went back to sleep. If that story is not true, it should be! We need to be aware, not afraid.

Be Filled with God's Spirit

Another piece of wisdom I have for you is this, and it's not really optional: If we're going to walk in God's freedom, we have to learn how to be filled with the Spirit of God. Stop the debate. Stop limiting what you invite Him to do. Humble yourselves. If you spoke in an uninviting way about Him, if you've mocked the Holy Spirit, if you've made fun of what you don't know, repent! We need His help!

In Ephesians, Paul writes:

> *Be very careful, then, how you live—not as unwise but as wise, making the most of every opportunity, because the days are evil. Therefore do not be foolish, but understand what the Lord's will is. Do not get drunk on wine, which leads to debauchery. Instead, be filled with the Spirit, speaking to one another with psalms, hymns, and songs from the Spirit.*

Sing and make music from your heart to the Lord, always giving thanks to God the Father for everything, in the name of our Lord Jesus Christ.

EPHESIANS 5:15-20

In that passage, Paul shows the behaviors that flow out of being filled with the Spirit. He tells us to speak God's Word and encourage each other with hymns and songs, to sing praises to the Lord, and to always give thanks to God.

He does not say, "Talk to one another at length about what you just read online or heard on your favorite news channel." The Church has been too carnal for too long. We've imagined our future was secured by things other than God so we have become a little sloppy and lazy. We can't afford that any longer.

To summarize, here's our strategy so far:

- Remember, fighting evil is about a truth encounter.
- Be aware but not afraid of the spiritual realm.
- On a daily basis, consciously think about behaviors you can engage in that will fill you with God's Spirit.

Now I'd like to add another point: We need to cultivate the will to resist evil. This is not my idea—Peter himself told us this in his letters. When he wrote 1 and 2 Peter in the Bible, he was no longer the brash, young fisherman we met in the Gospels. It was the end of his life, and he'd been tempered by a great deal of life experience, ministering on the front line of the Church since Jesus' ascension.

Peter preached on the day of Pentecost (see Acts 2).

Peter was the one who was sent to the Gentiles the first time, when God directed him to go to Cornelius' home in Caesarea (see Acts 10).

Peter had to explain his actions—preaching to the Gentiles—to very agitated Jewish Christ-followers back in Jerusalem (see Acts 11).

Then, Peter had to yield a bit of the floor to the rising voice of Paul, the apostle to the Gentiles (see Acts 15). So, by the time we get to the letters he wrote, they're tempered by a lot of life, and he provides very valuable words to us.

Humble Yourself

In 1 Peter, chapter 5, verse 6, he writes: *"Humble yourselves, therefore, under God's mighty hand, that he may lift you up in due time."*

If you want to be promoted in the Kingdom of God, the doorway to promotion begins at humility. You can humble yourself, or you can be humiliated. I would encourage you to humble yourself.

Give Jesus Your Anxieties

First Peter, chapter 5, verse 7 continues, *"Cast all your anxiety on him because he cares for you."* Peter tells us not to be anxious.

There are things in the world and life circumstances that cause anxiety. I'm not denying it's real. I'm not suggesting you don't have reason. The instruction we're given is to give all that anxiety to the Lord. You cannot live an anxious life and listen to the Spirit of God at the same time.

Again, we're developing an exit strategy. How do we walk in peace, so centered in God's truth that no matter what happens in the earth, we land in the place God has for us, ready to accept an assignment and to make a difference? It starts with, *Cast all your anxiety on Him.*

This means you need a daily routine for offloading that anxiety. Recognize what causes it, and take those thoughts to the Lord.

You see, dwelling in God's peace requires the involvement of your thoughts. And the real focus, the bedrock of that, is a trust in the Lord. There's an interplay between trust, peace, and fear. Where fear is flourishing, our trust is diminished. If there are things that frighten you or that bring anxiety and uncertainty to you, you've found a place where you haven't yet established trust in the Lord. When you imagine that you can secure something, and your ability to secure it is threatened, it creates anxiety and fear. Rather than be ashamed, embarrassed, angry, or mad at God, began to say, "Lord, I realize there's a place here where I have not trusted You. I've been trusting in myself. Thank You for that awareness. Help me learn to trust You in this area. Holy Spirit, I need Your help."

Cultivate Self-Control

Verse 8 says, *"Be self-controlled and alert."*

Self-control is one of the fruits of the Spirit, and you have to intentionally cultivate it. Our culture diminishes the value of self-control. People say, "I can't deny how I feel!" That may be true, but you can also admit that what you're feeling is not good. We have all kinds of language that gives license to ungodliness, but what we're really doing is exposing ourselves to evil.

In his letter, Peter is encouraging us to "be self-controlled and alert," based on his life experiences and the direction of the Holy Spirit. He tells us why, as verse 8 continues: *"Your enemy the devil prowls around like a roaring lion looking for someone to devour."* You have a spiritual enemy that is far more deadly than the Taliban, Hamas, or COVID. Most people who contract COVID survive, but without Christ, no one subjected to the Devil's schemes survive them. He's a far more devastating enemy. Do you have a plan?

Resist the Devil and Submit to God

Verse 9 tells us what to do: *"Resist him, standing firm in the faith, because you know that the family of believers throughout the world is undergoing the same kind of sufferings."*

Suffering is universal, but one of the things suffering does when it touches your life is it tries to convince you that you're unique.

"Nobody has suffered the junk I've suffered." But the Bible tells us, "Resist the Devil, standing firm in the faith. Remember that you have brethren around the earth who are suffering, too."

Our assignment is to resist the Devil, and we see the promise in verse 10: *"And the God of all grace, who called you to his eternal glory in Christ, after you have suffered a little while, will himself restore you and make you strong, firm and steadfast."* This means we'll be better off in the end, after the suffering, than we were in the beginning. But the pathway is an intentional choice to resist—to choose to overcome evil with good.

Our job is to stand against evil every place God takes us—not just when it comes under our roof. This isn't just about you, your spouse, and your two kids—us four and no more. We're the light of the world and the salt of the earth. We are called to stand against evil in the earth. That's our assignment.

In 1 Peter, chapter 2, verse 9, the apostle told us, *"But you are a chosen people, a royal priesthood, a holy nation, God's special possession, that you may declare the praises of him who called you out of darkness into his wonderful light."* He's not just talking about praising God with me and my own. We're meant to share the good news with all people, showing them the distinctiveness of a life yielded to God.

We see a similar message in the book of James:

> *Submit yourselves, then, to God. Resist the devil, and he*

will flee from you. Come near to God and he will come near to you. Wash your hands, you sinners, and purify your hearts, you double-minded. Grieve, mourn and wail. Change your laughter to mourning and your joy to gloom. Humble yourselves before the Lord, and he will lift you up.

JAMES 4:7-10

Submitting yourself to the Lord is just the beginning. That's not just saying the Sinner's Prayer and being baptized. That's saying every day, "Lord, I'm going to submit to You today." We build our plans, and we want God to submit to our plans. We have our dreams and our intents, and they're not evil nor wicked, but we've got to be willing to submit them to God.

We often get mad at God, saying, "I don't like what You're doing. You're doing a lousy job of managing my plan. Have You not read it? I wanted to be at this position by this point. I wanted to have accumulated this money, or I wanted my children to be here in my city, or I wanted to be doing that job, and I'm mad at You."

Instead, we simply need to say, "Lord, I want to follow You today. More than anything else, I want to follow You."

Yield to God's Plans

The universe we live in shouts at us about the order and precision of our God. So, yielding to God's plans is not about living recklessly, without planning or structure. I'm talking about yielding your will to God. Do you have the courage to follow Him?

When I began to follow the Lord, I did not want to ask Him what He wanted me to do with my life. I spent years fasting, praying, and reading my Bible. I prayed for hours and hours, telling God what I wanted to do and asking Him to bless it. I remember the day that changed. I had just about finished my undergraduate work in college, and I had a few minutes after lunch. I sat down on a little day bed in my dorm room, leaned back against a concrete block wall, and picked up my Bible. I heard the Spirit of God say, "You can go." I knew exactly what He meant. I knew I had the freedom to do what I had been asking Him for, and God just said, "Okay. You go." It frightened me to my core because I understood I was a rebel. I knew I had never said to the Lord, "What would *You* like me to do?" because I didn't want to know.

I spent a few days walking around with that, and I knew I was standing at a fork in the road. My future would be determined by what I did next. I chose to follow the Lord onto a new path—His path—even though that meant changing degrees so I could still graduate on time. It took some extra hard work, and the path didn't become clear immediately. In fact, it was years later before it became clear, with some tremendous heartache in between—but it all began by yielding to Him.

Romans, chapter 13, verse 14, offers us additional insight: *"But put on the Lord Jesus Christ, and make no provision for the flesh, to fulfill its lusts"* (NKJV®). If you examine the military, you can see what provisions look like: beans and bullets. We make too much provision for our carnal selves. You know how to make plans to indulge yourself. You know what you hide from certain people so they don't know about it. The biblical instruction is to *"make no provision for the flesh."* If you want to give the flesh and your old, carnal, selfish nature less influence in your life, stop making provision for it.

You might say, "Well, I like it." Therein lies the rub.

You might say, "Don't you want me to be happy?" I'm not opposed to happiness, but I would encourage you toward holiness. When your desire for holiness eclipses your desire for happiness, you'll gain some momentum and freedom. It's not an either/or choice. Serving God doesn't make you less happy. Pursuing happiness apart from God makes it an idol.

Seven Steps to Spiritual Freedom

There are seven steps you can take to choose freedom in your life and stand strong against the forces of evil, and I want you to have them in your portfolio. Once you experience the freedom these steps bring, you can help somebody else find that freedom, too.* After each step, there is a sentence statement—a proclamation—to read aloud.

* To learn even more about finding spiritual freedom in your life, I highly recommend Neil T. Anderson's books, *The Bondage Breaker* and *The Steps to Freedom in Christ.*

The path to freedom begins by confessing your faith in Christ and His sacrifice on your behalf. Apart from this truth, we have no authority to be free. Apart from the freedom that is ours in Christ, we are under the dominion of Satan and his kingdom. That's what makes Jesus so essential for our world. That's why we have to preach the gospel to the whole world. Governments, economic upticks, and education will not bring freedom. Freedom comes to us—fundamentally and spiritually—through our faith in Jesus. That's the message of the Church!

STEP ONE

Confess your faith in Jesus as Lord of your life, and acknowledge the sacrifice He made on your behalf. Romans, chapter 10, verse 9 says, *"If you confess with your mouth the Lord Jesus and believe in your heart that God has raised Him from the dead, you will be saved"* (®NKJV).

Doing this is as simple as reading this prayer aloud with a sincere heart: **Lord Jesus Christ, I believe You are the Son of God and the only way to God, and You died on the cross for my sins and rose again from the dead. Amen.**

STEP TWO

Repent of all your rebellion and sins. The fundamental sin is our rebellion. In this step, you'll repent for any sin you are conscious of. To stay spiritually clean, you have to acknowledge your sin by saying, "God, I'm a sinner, please forgive me" on a regular basis. Don't stay guilty. Be aware that we have an enormous tendency to swerve off the path, and we need to regularly repent of all our rebellion and sins. In the very beginning of His ministry, Jesus said in Mark, chapter 1, verse 15, *"'The time has come,' he said. 'The kingdom of God has come near. Repent and believe the good news!'"*

One time, I was trying to help somebody who wanted to become a Christian. He was well-educated and sophisticated, with lots of life experience. I would explain the gospel to him, and he would say, "It just doesn't make sense to me." So, I'd try again, but I was making no progress, and so I stopped for a moment and said, "May I ask you a question? Have you ever been involved in the occult? Did you go to fortune tellers, read horoscopes, or ask for spiritual guidance from something other than the Holy Spirit?" He looked at me and said, "How did you know that?" And I said, "Would you be willing to repent and tell the Lord you're sorry?" And he said, "Well, I don't see what it would hurt." So, I led him in a simple little prayer, and I came back and said, "Now, let me tell you what Jesus did again." He began to cry, and then he said, "Jesus did that for me?"

You see, repentance opens your capacity to believe God. If you have a difficult time believing the Bible, believing who Jesus is, and cooperating with the Holy Spirit, ask God to show you what you need to repent of and if you've opened a door to something that is impeding your life. When you're ready, confess it to Him, and then read this prayer aloud: **I give up all my rebellion and all my sin, and I submit myself to You as my Lord.**

STEP THREE

Claim forgiveness of all sins. Sin is a far more challenging problem than we've acknowledged. We've lived with this idea of sloppy grace—when you make a series of wicked choices you knew were wrong, then afterward say, "Oh, I'm kind of sorry." That's not the proper response. Our sin doesn't just hurt us—it impacts other peoples' lives, too. We need to say, "God, I grieved You. I've made Your people vulnerable. I've opened the door for evil into lives beyond my own. God, I'm sorry."

Once you repent of your sin, you need to receive forgiveness. You also need to forgive yourself.

First John, chapter 1, verses 8 and 9 say, *"If we claim to be without sin, we deceive ourselves and the truth is not in us. If we confess our sins, he is faithful and just and will forgive us our sins and purify us from all unrighteousness."*

If you've acknowledged your sin and you've repented of it, let it go. It doesn't define you any longer. Hallelujah! This is part of the reason we serve God with such abandon. He's been good to us! I deserve judgment, but He has forgiven me. When the Devil reminds you what you did, you can tell him, "Get out of here! The Lord has forgiven me of that. That's not who I am any longer."

Here is our next one-sentence prayer to read aloud:

I confess all my sins before You and ask for Your forgiveness—especially for any sins that exposed me to a curse. Release me also from the consequences of my ancestors' sins. In Jesus' name, amen.

STEP FOUR

Forgive all the people who have harmed you or wronged you.

Think of unforgiveness like a pathogen or a disease. If you harbor unforgiveness, you give a destructive force liberty in your life. You'll never cause God to agree with you in your unforgiveness. There is no case so compelling that God will say, "Well, in that case, I think I'll just hate right along with you." You see, the one qualification for being forgiven is our willingness to forgive. Jesus tells us in Matthew, chapter 6, verses 14 and 15, "'*For if you forgive other people when they sin against you, your heavenly Father will also forgive you. But if you do not forgive others their sins, your Father will not forgive your sins.*'"

He gives us additional instruction in Mark, chapter 11, verse 25: "'*And when you stand praying, if you hold anything against anyone, forgive them, so that your Father in heaven may forgive you your sins.*'"

Forgiveness begins as a decision. It's not an emotion. Your

emotions will have to catch up. It's like when you decide you're going to eat healthier—your decision gets there long before the rest of you does. Your mind is saying, *I need a little less ice cream*, but the rest of you is screaming, "ICE CREAM!" It takes a while for your body to follow what your mind is telling it to do.

Forgiveness is like that. Your emotions will say, "You didn't really forgive *them*, did you?" And you'll say, "Yes, I did. That one evening in August, as I was reading that book, I forgave them."

Here's the one-sentence prayer to read aloud:

By a decision of my will, I forgive all who have harmed me or wronged me—just as I want God to forgive me. In particular, I forgive ____________________.

There are likely several names you'll put in there, and I'll tell you how to identify them: If there is a name or circumstance that comes to mind, and you feel an inner response, you need to forgive. If somebody is still eliciting an emotion from you from forty years ago and they are deceased, you still need to forgive them. Remember, this is about truth and freedom.

STEP FIVE

Renounce all contact with anything satanic or involving the occult.

The pursuit of any spiritual insight, guidance, or power other than from the Spirit of the Living God is destructive, and it opens a doorway into your life to unclean spirits and their activity. You might say, "I don't believe that." I know, that's why we're talking about it. We've lived with such lack of awareness. We've lived such spiritually reckless lives, it has diminished the Church's capacity to believe. We need to come back and begin to take God at His Word.

There's a passage in 2 Corinthians that is helpful. Chapter 6, verse 14 says, *"Do not be yoked together with unbelievers."* For decades, the Church in America has spent time figuring out how we could do precisely the opposite of that. I don't want us to be angry at unbelievers or condemning of them, but our lives are supposed to be different than theirs. How you spend your free time should be different. What you dream about should be different. Your aspirations for your children should be different than the unbelievers.

Paul's advice continues:

> *For what do righteousness and wickedness have in common? Or what fellowship can light have with darkness? What harmony is there between Christ and Belial? Or what does a believer have in common with an unbeliever? What agreement is there between the temple of God and idols? For we are the temple of the living God. As God has said: "I will live with them and walk among them, and I will be their God, and they will be my people." Therefore, "Come out from them and be separate, says the Lord. Touch no unclean thing,*

and I will receive you." And, "I will be a Father to you, and you will be my sons and daughters, says the Lord Almighty." Therefore, since we have these promises, dear friends, let us purify ourselves from everything that contaminates body and spirit, perfecting holiness out of reverence for God.

2 CORINTHIANS 6:14-7:1

These passages make it clear: We have to come out from amongst the unbelievers. We have to be delivered. We have to *want* to be free. We're wearing too much camouflage. We don't even want to be around people who are "too godly." We're not sure what to talk to them about. It feels awkward. We don't want to tell them what we're dreaming about. We don't want to tell them what we're excited about because we recognize, intuitively, we're standing in a different place. So, we get mad at them. We criticize them. We blame them. I've been there.

We're looking for a pathway to freedom. If you don't want freedom, you can ignore the pathway. If you want freedom, I encourage you to take it seriously and keep pursuing it.

Here is our one-sentence prayer to pray aloud: **I renounce all contact with the occult or anything satanic. I cancel all Satan's claims against me.**

STEP SIX

Pray a prayer of release from any curse.

Galatians, chapter 3, verse 13 says, *"Christ redeemed us from the curse of the law by becoming a curse for us, for it is written: 'Cursed is everyone who is hung on a pole.'"*

That statement certainly includes the forgiveness of your sins, but it's not limited to that initiation into the Kingdom of God. It also extends to any curse brought upon you by other people or by previous generations in your family, or curses that you inadvertently brought upon yourself.

Here is the next prayer:

Lord Jesus, I believe that on the cross You took on Yourself every curse that could ever come upon me. I ask You now to release me from every curse over my life—in Your name, Lord Jesus Christ! By faith I now receive my release, and I thank You for it.

STEP SEVEN

Believe that you have received, and go forward in God's blessing.

Your emotions will have to catch up with this because some of this stuff has been with you for such a long period of time that it's part of the fabric of your life. Some of you have been angry for so long, it's how people know you. People walk around you on eggshells, and you're kind of proud of it. You have never known a different way to be—but now that you have made the beginning steps toward being free, keep walking forward with the Lord.

Take these ideas and live with them. Meditate on them. The Spirit of God will begin to show you some ways to respond. Maybe He'll show you some people you owe an apology. Maybe there would be some things in your home you need to get rid of. You may have to change some habits or patterns and realign some relationships.

The question is this: To what extent are you willing to resist the Devil to choose freedom, or do you think you can accommodate all of your baggage and be okay? It's a decision to make. The spiritual world is real, and you can't accommodate evil and expect the Spirit of God to overcome what you're accommodating. We've got to do the part we've been asked to do. Here's one last sentence prayer to say aloud:

Lord, I now open myself to receive Your blessing in every way You want to impart it to me.

Here's a summary of all the statements we just worked through. You may want to read through them two or three times a day, every day, until you began to find a new freedom.

Lord Jesus Christ, I believe You are the Son of God and the

only way to God, and You died on the cross for my sins and rose again from the dead.

I give up all my rebellion and all my sin, and I submit myself to You as my Lord.

I confess all my sins before You and ask for Your forgiveness—especially for any sins that exposed me to a curse. Release me also from the consequences of my ancestors' sins.

By a decision of my will, I forgive all who have harmed me or wronged me—just as I want God to forgive me. In particular, I forgive ____________________.

I renounce all contact with the occult or anything satanic. I cancel all Satan's claims against me.

Lord Jesus, I believe that on the cross You took on yourself every curse that could ever come upon me. I ask You now to release me from every curse over my life—in Your name, Lord Jesus Christ! By faith I now receive my release, and I thank You for it.

Lord, I now open myself to receive Your blessing in every way You want to impart it to me.

I pray all of this in Jesus' name, amen.

19 CHAPTER NINETEEN

MOVING FORWARD

We are living in a season of discontinuity, a break with the past. I'm excited about what's ahead of us. I think God is moving, and I'm looking forward to that, but seasons of great change also bring feelings of weariness—physically and emotionally. It takes effort to maintain your balance and your equilibrium. You have to pay more attention, you have to think, and you have to process things you used to take for granted. But right alongside the discontinuity and change, we find an invitation to yield to God, allowing Him to use this season to grow our faith and our belief in Him.

Here are some practices to intentionally cultivate as we move forward:

- A meaningful prayer life

- An awareness and knowledge of the Word of God
- A willingness to meditate on what God has said
- Fellowship with other believers. Together, we can help one another watch, listen, and think about what's happening in the world around us.
- Hospitality
- A willingness to open our lives to God's invitations

Putting those foundations in place will provide the strength, knowledge, and insight we need to respond to our world and the spiritual conflict surrounding us. It's the preparation you and I must do to accept an assignment of significance in this season.

I interact with Christians across our nation on a regular basis, and as we endure this time of turmoil, everybody asks the same question: "What can we do?" Our tendency is to see the greater need and think, *That's not right! That shouldn't be happening! I have to do something!* We don't feel like we have access to powerful people or tremendous resources—or at least not enough resources to walk back what's happening—and so we feel impotent and frustrated, as if there's nothing we can do. But that's not true. It's a lie that comes from the pit, and it's supported by unclean spirits.

Focus on the Fundamentals

Here's what we can do: Choose not to lose the battle in your mind—don't give Satan any ground. Focus on the foundations above. Say, "God, I'm going to give more time to my Bible and to thinking about what it says. I'll give more time to prayer. I'll spend more time in community with like-minded believers. I'll open my life to practice hospitality to help others see what warm hospitality feels like. I'm going to invest in those fundamentals."

Now, the reason that matters is that God will issue you or me an assignment when we're prepared. He loves you too much to give you an assignment you're not prepared for. When we see needs and think, *God, aren't You going to raise up a voice?* God responds to us, "Why don't you get ready?"

Please don't imagine these fundamentals are insignificant or busy work. They are foundational. We need these practices in place, so we're prepared for what's ahead.

- We have to choose to forgive those who we need to forgive.
- We have to choose to put on the full armor of God.
- We have to choose to say no to ungodliness and yes to godliness.
- We have to choose to repent of our sin.
- We have to choose to put off the old self and put on the new self.
- We have to choose to be renewed in our mind.
- We have to choose, having done everything we know to do, to stand and say, "I won't yield to evil. I won't yield in my home, in the schools, or in my neighborhood."

If we will give attention to the fundamentals, God will use

simple people like you and me to make a significant difference in our world.

David took down Goliath, not because he recognized Goliath was a threat—the entire Israelite army saw that. When David heard Goliath, he heard something different than all the Israelite soldiers. He said, "Goliath has challenged the army of the Living God, and my God is a Deliverer. He delivered the lion and the bear into my hand." David had been practicing while he took care of sheep and nobody was watching, so he was ready for a different stage.

You may say, "God, I'm ready for a stage!" When God thinks you're ready, He'll give you the assignment. You don't get to pick the stage. Your job is to just get ready.

Preparation and Response

We see an example of what happens when we take time to nurture the fundamentals in Daniel, chapter 9. The Hebrew people were under God's judgment. They'd been driven out of Jerusalem, and Jerusalem had been destroyed—their homes were gone, they had no assets, and they were slaves in a foreign country. Daniel, because of his abilities, had been selected for court service.

In chapter 9, verse 1, Daniel tells us about an event that occurred, *"In the first year of Darius ...."* This statement gives us an historical marker—kind of like dropping a pin on a digital map.

Verse 2 continues, *"I, Daniel, understood from the Scriptures, according to the word of the LORD given to Jeremiah the prophet, that the desolation of Jerusalem would last seventy years."*

This verse points out that Daniel had been studying the scriptures and thinking about them. He wasn't just plugging through his fifteen minutes a day. He was actually studying, thinking, and applying himself to learning. Through all of that studying, he deduced that the Hebrews would only be gone from Jerusalem for seventy years. You may think that's simple, but the deportation from Israel to Babylon took place in more than one wave. So, it took some discernment and study to understand the timeline. Daniel told the people, "I see it! I see it! We can go home soon! We can go home soon!" Daniel didn't get on the banquet circuit and start charging for appearances. Instead, in verse 3 he says, *"So I turned to the Lord God and pleaded with him in prayer and petition, in fasting, and in sackcloth and ashes."*

God gave Daniel an assignment because he was doing the fundamentals. God could trust him with an assignment to pray and push back on the principalities and powers that were mistreating His people. We know that because the angel Gabriel shows up, and in verse 23 he says, *"'As soon as you began to pray, a word went out, which I have come to tell you, for you are highly esteemed. Therefore, consider the word and understand the vision.'"*

Daniel was prepared. Decide today to be a person prepared for an assignment.

Listen to the way Daniel prays in verses 4 and 5: *"I prayed to the LORD my God and confessed: 'Lord, the great and awesome God, who keeps his covenant of love with those who love him and keep his commandments, we have sinned and done wrong. We have been wicked and have rebelled; we have turned away from your commands and laws.'"*

Instead of being mad at politicians or political parties, we could be like Daniel and say, "Lord, we have sinned. We have done wrong. We have been indifferent. We've had godly people run for office, and we didn't support them because we didn't like them, they didn't comb their hair right, or they looked frumpy in their suits. Lord, we have done wrong, and we have not listened to Your servants."

Daniel was desperate in the midst of even good news, and God sent angels to help him. He will do the same for us, too.

Why do we avoid being desperate for the Lord? Why do we prefer to pretend like we're in control? I think it's because we don't understand enough to navigate the circumstances we're in. We know some things, but we don't know enough. We need God's help. If you don't think you need God's help, pray that God gives you a revelation of how much you actually do.

Then, when you recognize God has an invitation in front of you, treat it as the most precious thing in your life.

If He's showing you something to repent of, repent with enthusiasm.

If He's showing you a way to respond—if it's an expression of generosity, time, or a reordering of something—respond to Him. There's no guarantee you'll get a second invitation.

It's Training Season

We're in training. The Lord is waking us up! Isaiah, chapter 61 tells us to put on the garment of praise instead of the spirit of despair. We don't want to give any place to a spirit of despair. We want the Spirit of the Lord to know He's welcome in our lives, and that we're grateful for what He's done for us. He has called us out of darkness and rescued us from the kingdom of darkness. I was behind enemy lines far worse than the Taliban, and the Lord came and got me, and you, too—not because we deserved it, or we were good enough, or we could afford it, or He needed us—but because He loved us.

From Genesis all the way through Revelation, God's people are constantly learning, listening, and being invited to change and grow. We're not changing the essence of what we believe—those things are non-negotiable. But *how* we live out our faith in the world requires us to respond to the challenges of this generation.

There's a purpose in reading your Bible, learning to pray, meditating on Scripture, and practicing obedience. They're not just mindless deeds meant to be completed as a checklist. They teach us how to listen. They help us learn to trust the God of Abraham, Isaac, and Jacob, and yield to Him in our own lives. They help us discern God's voice and His truth from the lies of the enemy. If we take these fundamentals seriously, when we're given an assignment and invited to participate, we'll be ready to take our places.

The good news is we are never alone. The angels and God's Spirit are ready to come alongside us, encourage us, strengthen us, and help us complete the assignment. We simply need to acknowledge their existence and welcome their help—it's clear we desperately need it!

LET'S PRAY

Heavenly Father, I thank You and praise You that I've been delivered and redeemed. I worship You because, through the blood of Jesus, I have been set free from the power of the enemy—he has no authority over me, no place in me, and no dominion over me. I praise You that You're the strength of my body. You're the peace in my mind. You're the hope in my soul. I worship You. You are worthy of all glory, honor, praise, and thanksgiving. I need Your mercy, and I cry out to You because You're a merciful God. Pour out Your Spirit upon me and send Your angels to come alongside me and protect me. Forgive me for my stubbornness, rebellion, and indifference. Give me listening ears and a receptive heart so I will respond to You with a willing spirit. I love You, and I praise You. In Jesus' name, amen.

Notes

Notes

Notes

Notes

Notes

Notes

Notes

Notes

Notes

Notes

Notes

Notes

Notes

Notes

Notes

Notes

Notes

Notes

Notes

Notes

Notes

Notes

For more from Allen Jackson—including sermons, books, podcasts, and small group studies—visit:

allenjackson.com